Sacred
Relationship

Heart Work for Couples

ANNI DAULTER
and TIM DAULTER

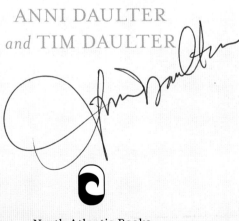

North Atlantic Books
Berkeley, California

Published by
North Atlantic Books
Berkeley, California

Cover photo by Sarah Loven of Ready Gypset Go
Cover design by Claudia Smelser
Interior design by Claudia Smelser, Jasmine Hromjak, and Happenstance Type-O-Rama

Printed in the United States of America

Sacred Relationship: Heart Work for Couples is sponsored and published by the Society for the Study of Native Arts and Sciences (dba North Atlantic Books), an educational nonprofit based in Berkeley, California, that collaborates with partners to develop cross-cultural perspectives, nurture holistic views of art, science, the humanities, and healing, and seed personal and global transformation by publishing work on the relationship of body, spirit, and nature.

North Atlantic Books' publications are available through most bookstores. For further information, visit our website at www.northatlanticbooks.com or call 800-733-3000.

LIBRARY OF CONGRESS CATALOGING-IN-PUBLICATION DATA

Names: Daulter, Anni, author. | Daulter, Tim, author.
Title: Sacred relationship : heart work for couples : daily practices and
   inspirations for a deeper connection / Anni Daulter, Tim Daulter.
Description: Berkeley, California : North Atlantic Books, 2017.
Identifiers: LCCN 2017006333| ISBN 9781623171209 (paperback) | ISBN
   9781623171216 (ebook)
Subjects: LCSH: Marriage--Psychological aspects. | Interpersonal relations. |
   Self-actualization (Psychology) | Love. | BISAC: FAMILY & RELATIONSHIPS /
   Marriage. | SELF-HELP / Personal Growth / Happiness. | PSYCHOLOGY / Human
   Sexuality.
Classification: LCC HQ503 .D38 2017 | DDC 306.8--dc23
LC record available at https://lccn.loc.gov/2017006333

1 2 3 4 5 6 7 8 9 VERSA 22 21 20 19 18 17

North Atlantic Books is committed to the protection of our environment. We partner with FSC-certified printers using soy-based inks and print on recycled paper whenever possible.

This is a book for all couples—not just those living in struggle, but all who want to live in high-vibration relationships and to do better and be better for each other and the world. It is also dedicated to my beloved, who has been my mirror, my rock, my heart, and my champion for many years. To say I love you barely scratches the surface of how my heart longs for you, so know that while I search for the best words to express my connection to you, I will just be here, ever-present and fully committed to our shared dreams.

~ANNI

I dedicate this book to love! For it was love that brought my soulmate to me. It was love that brought four wonderful children into my life. Every moment of happiness, every smile, and every belly laugh has been a gift from love. I wish for every reader of this book to be able to share the kind of love that has blessed me. My gratitude to you, Anni, is unfathomable, for without your love, support, guidance, forgiveness, and grace I would not be the man I am today.

~TIM

CONTENTS

INTRODUCTION

Welcome to *Sacred Relationship*, the book! We appreciate and honor your willingness to raise your love relationship to a higher level and share that awareness in the world. This is important not only because your love relationship is the center of your life—and key to your own personal happiness—but because this heart work will also serve as an example to your children, family, and friends. We define "sacred" as something that is of or connected to the Divine and is worthy of reverence and respect. When you treat your beloved and your relationship as sacred, you are literally changing the world.

The material and basis for this book are extensions of the Sacred Relationship live retreats (*www.oursacredrelationship.com*) that we have developed as part of the larger Sacred Living Movement (*www.sacredlivingmovement.com*). These retreats are held at various locations all over the world, and allow couples the space, for four uninterrupted days, to learn directly from us how to elevate their vibration, both separately and collectively, fall back into trust and heartfelt love with one another, get ooey-gooey romantic again, and learn practices to take home that will have positive effects on every aspect of their lives.

The approaches and techniques that you will learn in this book came directly from our own personal experience as individuals and as a couple who struggled and found our way out of a dark place into the brilliant light of a truly sacred connection with one another. Our relationship has gone through its ups and downs and—after ten years of marriage, four kids, and several entrepreneurial ventures—had fallen into such a state of neglect that we almost lost it. With the gifts of spiritual inspiration, we decided to make changes in our personal spiritual daily practices, how we thought about each other, how we talked to each other, and how we treated each other.

We did a lot of healing, and created a new relationship with a focused intention on love and living in our higher selves. The work of this book begins with the hope that you will look at your relationship with fresh eyes; then it moves into taking a deep drink of healing and releasing old wounds; finally, it encourages you to develop a set of simple daily practices that can profoundly transform your love relationship, and your life as a whole.

HOW TO USE THIS BOOK

This book is meant to be used as a relationship course for both of you. You should take the topics in order, from Week 1–32, and focus on no more than one topic per week. This time is needed for you to discuss the content with your beloved, do the suggested practices, and integrate the learning before moving on to the next week. There is an expansive difference between intellectual knowing and experiential knowing. Sitting and reading all of the information in the book can be a good start, but the real change in your life will come from doing the practices and integrating the heart-work changes into the way that you feel, think, and act.

For each lesson, we suggest that you and your beloved start your week by sitting separately and reading the chapter. It may be convenient for you to get an additional copy so that each of you has your own. Once you have both read the chapter, talk it through together to see what insights, thoughts, or feelings came up for you. Afterward, make a conscious plan to try some of the suggested Ideas and Practices and explore some of the Pairings during the week.

Make sure to regularly connect with each other on how it's going and what changes you are feeling. Keep in mind that there are *individual and couple* components of the book, so that each of you is working on yourself as well as reigniting or elevating your love spark. At the end of the week, come together again to review the heart work you have done and perform the journaling exercise together.

One powerful aspect of our Sacred Relationship live retreats is doing the work in community with other like-minded couples. So your experience would be even more enhanced if you could get together with a few other couples who are interested in working through the book at the same time. You can set up a weekly "book club" meeting to socialize and share your experiences each week. You can learn so much from hearing what other couples are going through, and this is a good way to stay motivated to do the work.

In the end, you are the deciding factor in the transformation and evolution of your relationship. This book contains information, insights and practices that have transformed many relationships and many lives. However, this can only happen if you are committed to positive change, if you enter with an open mind in perfect love and perfect trust and, most importantly, if you take the heart-work action that is suggested.

Perhaps we will see you at a Sacred Relationship live retreat one day; until then, take up this work as if you are the guru of love, and allow for intentional love, chosen in conscious awareness, to unfold into every aspect of your life. Change is not easy, and it takes an investment of time and energy—but the payoff for you, your beloved, your family, and everyone who touches your life is tremendous.

We wish you the best of luck, and send you our loving support!

~Anni and Tim Daulter

SECTION ONE

WE

Reflect

LOVE IS AWAKENING

Awaken, sweet lovers, from the stagnant slumber you have been in; rest, and begin to see with new eyes and open hearts.

Awaken, sweet lovers.

Stretch your limbs in new ways as you peek through the looking-glass of days past and set new intentions for love to bloom.

Begin again, sweet lovers.

Love is the tonic to all life's ailments; it is the highest calling and the most honorable house in which to dwell.

Live there, sweet lovers.

Sacred Relationships are crafted with care, sculpted with high vibration, and sustained with heart work.

Be dedicated, sweet lovers.

Release past ailments with a compassionate anecdote, and see the way beyond pain and suffering through empathy.

Be your best selves, sweet lovers.

Take one step, then another, then another. Lean into love, and hold each other up as you begin this very sacred journey.

Be love warriors, sweet lovers.

Swoon

where it all began

It was not into my ear you
whispered, but into my
heart. It was not my lips
you kissed, but my soul.

~JUDY GARLAND

And so it begins. It's always good to start a journey with an open heart and an ability to look back in order to see how to move forward. When you and your beloved met, everything was coming up roses. Nothing either of you did really bothered the other; behavioral nuances got overlooked for the greater good, and all you likely wanted to do was drink in every moment with each other, enjoying every subtle flavor of the love potion you were both guzzling down.

We call this the "cupid phase" of the relationship, and it serves one purpose—*to bring you together.* We believe that two people who are meant to be together—who share a soul contract with one another—are thrown together with a very strong attractive force for a reason. You cannot know the full measure of that Sacred Purpose in the beginning, but with each smile, each kiss, and each "I love you more than anything in the world," the seeds are being planted to fulfill this karmic path.

YOURSELF

The first step in setting up a Sacred Relationship is simply to decide that you want one. Ask yourself in a deep and truthful way whether you truly want a Sacred Relationship with your beloved, and your answer will help you begin with honesty. If you were drawn to this book, there is a reason for that, and if you can jump in with two feet and really give it a heartfelt go, you have a shot at reshaping your love to reflect a deeper, more meaningful relationship than you ever had in the past.

Here's the rub—it's gonna take a lot of dedication and heart work to make it worth the effort. So it's imperative that you both agree to walk this journey and try on the practices that we suggest throughout the book, with your most noble intentions. Start this journey with remembering how you fell in love. Each of you should take time to reflect on those cupid days, and remember with warm fuzzies in your hearts how you started. Talk about your first date over a good meal, and start reflecting on those yummy days of falling in love.

THE COUPLE

For your relationship to flourish and grow, you must find ways to live in your full awareness, make conscious decisions, say YES every day, and live in "right action" so that you can support your connection with your beloved and preserve its potential longevity. We call this stage "intentional love." This is a mature love, very different from obsessive love because it holds at its core the health of each individual and becomes the heartbeat of the couple.

Intentional love will bring more and deeper happiness, joy, and fulfillment than the initial love spell. It can slingshot you into personal growth while still honoring your relationship. This is the place we hope you will attain as you work your way through the practices and stay dedicated to the cause.

HEART WORK: *Understanding Right Action*

"Right action" is a concept that often takes years to accomplish, but one you can take up as a daily practice, working toward it with the passionate heart of a master. Moving through life in right action means that you live every day in your full awareness, choosing with purpose and intention in every moment for the greatest good to always and in all ways be upheld. Right action means striving to live in a proactive, loving state of heart rather than a reactive, unconscious state of mind. Right action means that you want your beloved to feel good, and that may mean letting go of determining who is right and wrong.

Start with a five-minute meditation, clearing your mind of all junk and stress, stating your purpose of wanting to live the day in full presence of heart, and allow love to rule your words.

Throughout the day, speak with a kind tone; do not let the concerns of the day filter into your presence with the poisons of stress or anxiety. If something bothers you, choose love instead of anger. Love is life's medicine and cures all, so when you live from a place of love you are acting from right action and divine mind rather than reacting from old tapes of childhood or past hurts. As we said, this takes a lot of practice to master, but it's a goal worth attaining both for you personally and for the collective good of the relationship.

IDEAS AND PRACTICES

Create a Sacred Space

As you move through this book, it is important for you to have a sacred spot in your home to spend time meditating alone, doing heart-to-heart meditations together, journaling, and creating.

Choose a space in your home that has good vibes and just feels right to both of you. It should have an empty shelf or small side table available where both of you can add special items that reflect your relationship, such as an "intentions candle," fresh flowers, crystals, stones, and other special items that mean something to you both— old love letters, a picture of the two of you, some incense, sage, or essential oils that smell nice—and you can keep this book there too. This will serve as your Relationship Love Altar, and should be cleaned and maintained on a regular basis.

An altar provides energetic focus to your intentions and starts beautifying your commitment to your love. This can be a good space to leave love notes, small gifts, or other surprises for your beloved. As you move through these pages, we will ask you to take up practices that will always and in all ways need to start with a clear mind and devoted heart. This sacred space can help you drop into that place within you and bring focus to your daily heart work. We encourage you to build this Love Altar together, spending time there daily, and lighting your intentions candle to set the day for a high-vibration outcome.

Scribe your love story

The thing about your love story that makes it inherently special is that it only belongs to the two of you. It is a sacred moment in time that was formed and likely shaped by long phone calls, romantic dates, make-out sessions, and delicate moments that only you two share. It is so important to remember those days and honor them!

It may be that the two of you remember your love story differently, so take time to individually scribe this time in your relationship and share it with each other. You can write it in the form of a love letter entitled, "How I fell in love with you," and leave it for the other to find on your Love Altar. This reflecting will help you both to soften and to begin this journey with an open heart.

pairings

- Intentions candle mantra: choose a candle for your Love Altar and, when you light it for the first time, state your intentions. For example, "We are lighting this candle to help grow our relationship in light and love." Use this mantra or create one of your own that you can use to set your intention every time you light the candle. Choose a white or pink candle to represent pure love.
- Song: "My Love" by Nina Lee.

Journal on Swoon

Use this space to scribe each of your versions of your love story, and to write down your intentions-candle mantra.

_____

_____

_____

_____

_____

_____

_____

_____

_____

_____

_____

_____

_____

_____

Soul Contracts

how you came together

The big-picture purpose of
a Soul Contract is to master its
lesson; the big picture of your
Soul Purpose is to align with
it and let it guide you.

~DANIELLE MACKINNON

The inertia that brings two people together in the beginning of a relationship is like an unstoppable train that only those two people are riding. Whether you met your beloved through a friend, locked eyes across a room, bumped shoulders walking down the street, or met on a dating website, the universe collided with your destinies in order to shove a Soul Contract in your face, saying "Sign on the dotted line!" There are bigger forces at play when it comes to romantic connections; otherwise you would just be in love with anyone at any time.

The soul contract that was written for the two of you exists because only your pairing is creating the perfect song to add to the Sacred Wheel of life. Perhaps the two of you are meant to create a beautiful heart-vision together that you must share with the world, or bring babies Earthside that are simply meant to be here, or to be each other's greatest teachers. You cannot know where the train will end up; all you know now is that there will be many magical stops along the way.

YOURSELF

The concept of soul contracts means that you made some agreements before coming to this earthly plane to help you evolve your spiritual destiny and elevate your soul closer to Source. You have free will within the framework of your destined connections, so some contracts will only have a short run while others will span several years or even lifetimes together, depending on the work and the willingness of each person to do it.

You were also sent here with spirit guides to help you find and follow your path, and you will know them by the clues and signs they illuminate in everyday life. For example, you may see recurring number sequences such as 11:11 or 12:44; or various synchronicities will unfold that will be noticeable and stop you in your tracks. These are good omens that your heart prayers are being heard and that you are on your soul path in this lifetime.

Take a moment to think back to the beginning of your relationship with your beloved. How did you meet? Was there anything that could have stopped the two of you from being together? Your soul contract with each other is a part of the greater plan, and thus needs to honored for the destined work you are meant to do together.

THE COUPLE

While there is no greater beauty than being in deep relationship with someone, it can also stir up the wellsprings of discomfort, open wounds from past days or lifetimes, or illuminate dysfunctional energy patterns that lie below the surface. Soul contracts are made between two lovers so that they can work out the demons and elevate themselves to the next level of spiritual advancement. This is a grand journey that may take several lifetimes, but the more you are able to work out with your beloved now, the more ease you will have matriculating forward.

You may have felt you have known each other for lifetimes, even on the first date, and that is very likely. Those feelings are triggered to initiate the soul contract's work, and understanding divine timing will help you move quickly into understanding the purpose of your relationship. Only the two of you have the inside scoop as to when the contract between you is up. The information lives in your cellular memory and your bones, so you will "feel it" and have a clear knowing of what steps you should take.

For now, breathe into trust. Find comfort knowing that you are both exactly where you need to be.

HEART WORK: *It's Soul–Amazing*

There is purpose to every relationship, and sitting down with your beloved to have a conversation about purpose and spiritual evolution can really bring some awareness to the energy patterns that you have played out with each other thus far. Unwrapping what each other believes is the primary purpose, so your coming together can be eye-opening and turn into a soul-amazing experience.

IDEAS AND PRACTICES

Make a list

Make a list of all the dysfunctional energy patterns that exist between you and your beloved. What mind games do you play with one another, and what emotional swords are drawn in your battles? The only way to dispel dysfunction is to shine light on the shadow parts. When you do this, try to have no emotional charge during this quest; simply write it as if you were putting milk and eggs on your grocery list, giving voice to the patterns that each of you sees as detrimental to both your individual growth and the health of your couplehood.

Living out soul contracts and elevating to the next step of spiritual enlightenment is completed when patterns are broken and new challenges are taken. Once you have learned a lesson from your guides, you are out of the old loop and catapulted to the next level.

SOUL-AMAZING SPRITZER

This spritzer can help you ground and connect into your spirit guides when you need help.

- 2-ounce spritzer bottle
- 2 ounces witch hazel
- 10 drops frankincense essential oil
- 10 drops sandalwood essential oil
- 5 drops sweet orange essential oil

Mix all ingredients in a bowl. Put mixture in bottle. Hold the bottle and set intentions for its use, including tapping into your soul purpose.

Shake well before use. Spritz everyday as you ground yourself, avoiding contact with eyes.

pairings

- Crystal: rock crystal quartz. This crystal is the most powerful on Earth, and can help you connect directly to Source. Its properties are healing and divine connection. Wear it on your person, or keep it in your Sacred Space.

- Card Deck: *The Soul's Journey Lesson Cards: A 44-Card Deck and Guidebook* by James Van Praagh.

Journal on Soul Contracts

Use this space to unravel your thoughts on the purpose of your relationship with your beloved. What energetic patterns are you working through?

_____

_____

_____

_____

_____

_____

_____

_____

_____

_____

_____

_____

_____

_____

_____

Heart Work

no greater purpose than love

Love is a symbol of eternity.
It wipes out all sense of time,
destroying all memory of a
beginning and all fear of an end.

~UNKNOWN

In the first week, the concept of heart work was brought to the table, but it requires diving deeper to understand how to properly unpack that concept into actionable daily tasks and find the treasure. To maintain a lasting long-term relationship filled with mutual respect, romance, joy, and high vibration is nothing short of a love miracle; this quest requires that you claim a bright and shiny superpower that you may have to call upon every single day. There will be dragons, thorns, fires, demons, shadows, and other scary shit to vanquish throughout your time shared with each other—and you can only do that armed with love, compassion, joy, and empathy.

So, yeah, no problem—right? Even masters take years to arm themselves with blades of purity such as these! So be patient with yourself, and know that with dedication, daily practice, and a whole lotta forgiveness you can take up heart work, become your own guru, and be a guiding light for what a true Sacred Relationship can be.

YOURSELF

Heart work is not only a cause worth pursuing for your beloved; it is the greatest gift you can give yourself. Think of what your life would look like if you lived only from love and shared only joy—if you were utterly truthful, compassionate, and empathetic to all beings around you. You would be a guru of epic proportions, likely floating and shooting rainbows from your eyes! However, precisely because these are such lofty goals, they should be pursued.

The definition of heart work is anything done with daily intention and discipline, and with your heart invested in the outcome. Building a Sacred Relationship is heart work that requires focus, commitment, and surrender to tender places within yourself, allowing the other to see your vulnerabilities and witness the moments when you are not 100 percent on your game. This is scary for many people because they fear that if they are seen as raw and real they may not be loved and accepted.

Saying YES to heart work serves you in the highest ways possible. It feeds you so that you can forgive transgressions rather than holding onto them in your spirit body. It helps you bow in reverence to joy, so that you are not bound to the demons of anger and low vibration. It serves you to BE LOVE, pushing fear aside and standing tall amongst the giants of love masters. All of this brings you to a place where you can shake hands with your highest self, look her in the eyes, and know you are your true soul's purpose on this Earth.

THE COUPLE

Always have the back of your beloved. If you keep this sentiment in your conscious awareness, you will be more capable of being of service to your love. Being of service is an honor when you both take it up with reverence and with the intention that unconditional love is your heart work—the greatest calling there is.

How do you know when you have exhausted the heart work, when the relationship needs to transition to a new definition, perhaps becoming friends instead of lovers? The answer lives only in your heart, and when you bring more daily practices to your life it will become clearer each day. "You will know" is the short of it.

If you are clear that your soul contract with one another is still going strong, then commit to doing the heart work with discipline and with truth on your lips. This work is the only way to a Sacred Relationship, so travel the road and experience each stop along the way, never getting discouraged by detours but welcoming them as part of the adventure.

HEART WORK: *Set Intentions*

In order to truly begin the journey of forming a Sacred Relationship, you must set right intentions to do so. Cleansing yourself of negative baggage from the past and your old wounds is a great place to start.

Ask Spirit to hold your hand down this path. Seeking signs and downloads from the Great Mystery as you navigate your new love roadmap will be essential to your success. This means, however, that if you are asking for help from the other side, you must do your part—stay awake in your life, pay attention to the signs, meditate so your mind is fresh and pure, stay in high vibration so you are radiating positive energy into the world, and infuse your relationship with the four pillars of true connection—love, compassion, joy, and empathy. Set these as your daily intentions, and you will create the necessary space for miracles to unfold.

IDEAS AND PRACTICES

See below for daily practices that will help you set and fulfill your heart-work intentions.

POLISH-YOUR-HEART LOVE OIL

At our Sacred Relationship live retreats, couples create a Polish-Your-Heart Love Oil together. The purpose of this oil is to literally polish each other's heart area, as a daily practice, while saying what you are grateful for about the other.

- 4-ounce glass jar with a lid
- 3 ounces base oil such as almond, avocado, or grapeseed
- various herbs and essential oils that speak to you both as a couple. You can add anything that appeals to your senses and has meanings that suit your relationship needs. Here is a short list of just a few herbs and oils, and their meanings:
- calendula—represents healing
- dried roses—represents love
- dried lavender—represents calm
- patchouli essential oil—activates the oil and helps sexual energies to rise
- sage essential oil—good for cleansing
- frankincense essential oil—used to connect with spirit and meditation
- sweet orange essential oil—used as a refreshing uplift
- rosemary essential oil—enhances focus, concentration, and protection

Fill up your jar about three-quarters full with your base oil, and then add dried herbs and essential oils. When you get the oil smelling the way you both like it, you are done. Mix and seal it.

Name your oil with the energy of the intention you are infusing into it.

This is a practice you can take up and enjoy every day: polish each other's heart area with your oil, and tell each other one thing you are grateful for in them. This fosters connection, appreciation, and a growing love between you.

LOTUS MUDRA MEDITATION

A mudra is a hand prayer that helps open up energy within your spirit body to commune with the Divine. Mudras represent various things, as evidenced in the many positions portrayed by Buddha's hands in statues. This one is called the Lotus Mudra; it helps you stay open, like the lotus flower, to your higher self.

- Sit in a quiet, beautiful space—perhaps in front of your Sacred Relationship Love Altar; light a candle and put on some nice, calming meditation-type music (such as Mary Isis's "Cosmic Bliss").

- Put your hands together in front of your heart in the traditional prayer pose. Keeping the bases of your hands touching, open the top of your hands in a petal-like position, with only pinkies and thumbs touching each other.

- Close your eyes and ask your divine guides to help you stay open to all possibility, and to give you the resolve to stay true to your heart work.

- Sit in this pose as long as it feels needed.

You can do this practice every day, and each time you need a touchstone reminder of your resolve.

pairings

- Rose-quartz crystal water. Rose quartz crystals represent love and joy. When your intention is to take up heart work, this can assist you in keeping your daily vibes high and your heart pure. Water holds the qualities of crystals well, so simply place a large piece of rose quartz into your drinking water. Every time you drink it, say a loving mantra to yourself such as, "With every sip, I am pure love." Doing this multiple times throughout the day will help you maintain focus and be more mindful of your daily actions.

- Rose-quartz *mala*. You can make or buy a rose-quartz mala, which is a prayer necklace with 108 beads that intersect with your chakra lines, and a holy bead at the end of the necklace that intersects with your heart chakra. Infuse this necklace with a mantra—a short and succinct statement that you can say over and over again to remind you to stay pure in your heart work. An example might be "I am love"—just a simple phrase that you can repeat throughout the day, so that the mala becomes a physical representation of your noble quest.

Journal on Heart Work

Each of you can use this space to make a list of your sacred intentions for building your relationship into its highest vibration. What are your grand visions for your connection? Are you disciplined enough to make it happen?

_____

_____

_____

_____

_____

_____

_____

_____

_____

_____

_____

_____

_____

_____

Beginner's Mind

see your beloved as if for the first time

In the beginner's mind

there are many possibilities....

~SHUNRYU SUZUKI

Beginner's Mind is an attitude and a choice. It is a willingness to let go of
everything you think you know about love, about relationships, about yourself,
and about your beloved. It is never too late to question your own thought patterns
and open up to new knowledge, ideas, and ways of looking at things.

Taking a Beginner's Mind attitude is a first and necessary step in changing how you feel in your relationship. When you acknowledge that there may be different ways to understand your relationship and your beloved, you create a crack in the edifice that traps your relationship at its current level. Creating this new space will allow you to think, act, and feel differently—in ways that allow you to expand into an entirely new level of relationship bliss.

YOURSELF

Choosing to live in Beginner's Mind is saying YES to personal freedom. We are all programmed with our own beliefs and expectations about relationships—they come from what we saw in our own parents, fairy tales, movies, and even commercials on television! Ultimately, at some point in our relationship, we will focus on what we are not getting from our beloved that we think we are entitled to receive.

This is an opportunity for each of us as individuals to take a look at our own deep expectations: what do we think we should be getting from our beloved, and what do we think we are required to give? *Then we need to shatter the idea that this is how it must be.*

At this point, open yourself to the possibility that everything that you have learned or think you know about relationships is wrong! Start slowly, and be open to the "What if . . .?" Once you do that, you will be ready to learn something new, see things differently, and create a new level of relationship that feels more wonderful, warm, and loving than ever.

THE COUPLE

The state of your current connection has evolved because of the attitudes, expectations, and beliefs that each of you brought to your union. The longer you have been together, the more solidified your expectations of each other have become, and these expectations create shackles that keep you in your current patterns. Break these bonds by letting go of all of your thoughts that begin with the following:

- My beloved never . . .
- My beloved always . . .
- I need my beloved to . . .
- My beloved doesn't care about . . .

Make the choice to loosen your grip on these thought patterns, and let in the possibility that you may not fully understand, or that there could be a different interpretation of what you see, hear, and feel. When you start to shift your thoughts on how you "know" your beloved will act and how you "know" your relationship will be, both you and your beloved will feel it. Space will begin to form, freedom from past patterns will emerge, and a new feeling of lightness will infuse your day.

HEART WORK: *Open to Seeing Anew*

Remember that the true meaning of your relationship is for you and your beloved to come together at the soul level to support the spiritual evolution of both each other and all those around you. The amazing experiences that you were born to share with each other require personal evolution, and that kind of growth requires openness to new ways of thinking and seeing.

Living in Beginner's Mind is an absolute necessity to a joyful and fulfilling life. When we become too rigid, thinking that we know everything, stagnation sets in and poisons our happiness, fulfillment, and inner peace. As growth-seeking beings, we must be flexible in how we view ourselves, and embrace the ever-changing flow of our lives. In relationship, we must also gift this flexibility and freedom to our beloved, so that the bond can expand and contract as time goes on.

Do not wait for your beloved to give this to you first. You take the action. You give the gift. You open your mind, because every gift that you give to your beloved you also give to yourself.

IDEAS AND PRACTICES

Identifying the hurt that causes pain in your relationship

The next time that you and your beloved drop into a negative pattern of communication—whether an argument, passive-aggressive behavior, or the good old-fashioned silent treatment—take a moment. Right then and there, stop saying anything negative about them to yourself or to them.

Consider that your beloved is only expressing negativity because they are feeling hurt inside. Try to understand the source of the hurt; show compassion, and try to see the entire situation from a different perspective. Anything that you can do to help heal your beloved's hurt will come back to you tenfold.

SEEING THROUGH NEW EYES

This is an exercise that you can do with any disagreement, big or small, in your relationship. You may want to start with the big, obvious issues plaguing you, to create room for a significant shift in your relationship.

- Take some quiet time by yourself to be in a meditative or contemplative state. Sit in a relaxed posture (but not if you are extremely tired or likely to fall asleep).

- In your mind's eye, think about the issue or disagreement living most deeply in you at this time. Take a moment to review your thoughts and feelings on this issue, and the position that you have staked out on it.

- Then consider for a moment that you are completely wrong. Come up with as many reasons as you can that could cause you to be wrong. If you have been thinking that you and your beloved need to live on a strict budget, think now about all the reasons you might want freedom and flexibility instead. If you think you need to move across the country to be closer to family, think instead of all of the potential possibilities and opportunities that you might miss by leaving where you are.

- Take some time to write down all the reasons why your usual position might be completely misguided.

- Consider some possibilities for moving forward with your beloved so that you could weave both perspectives into a more balanced space. See if you can find the treasure—a win/win rather than a lose/win solution.

pairings

- Crystal: azurite-malachite crystals can be very powerful in supporting your work to return to Beginner's Mind. Azurite is known to release mental stress and negative thoughts from your mind, allowing you to see things in a new way. And malachite is a great activator for transformation and healing. You can find stones containing this mixture and wear them in a necklace, keep one on your altar, or carry one in your pocket.

Journal on Beginner's Mind

Use this space to journal about where your thought patterns are stuck, and how you might open to new possibilities.

_____

_____

_____

_____

_____

_____

_____

_____

_____

_____

_____

_____

_____

_____

Pillow Talk

listen, understand, acknowledge

The biggest communication
problem is that we listen to respond
rather than to understand.

~UNKNOWN

It is widely said that communication is the cornerstone of a strong relationship. While this is true, most of us don't know how to nurture and manifest effective communication in our relationship. Communication is about more than just expressing yourself to your beloved, especially when you are upset with something.

While many people have trouble sharing their thoughts, what we see more often is that people feel they actually *do* express themselves, but that their beloved doesn't get it, or doesn't seem to care. The work here is twofold: 1) express yourself truthfully, and don't hold things inside; and 2) learn to be able to hear, understand, and acknowledge your beloved's thoughts, feelings, and dreams.

YOURSELF

Learning to listen is often the most difficult part of improving communication with your beloved. The main block here is ego—if your beloved is expressing hurt, dissatisfaction or desire for change, it is easy to personalize their comment and take it as a criticism. When feeling criticized, you tend to switch from open mode to defensive mode and then use denial, counter-criticism, or some other technique to "protect" yourselves. When this happens, the possibility for communication is destroyed.

You need to be able to move out of your ego and listen to your beloved. Do not take anything said as a criticism, but focus only on hearing what they feel, what desires they are expressing, and the lens through which they are experiencing your relationship. When you can truly listen in this way, you will be able to understand your beloved and where they are coming from.

THE COUPLE

Over time, all couples develop habits in their communication. Each couple has a unique set of difficult subjects. These can range from a place where everything is difficult to one where just a few subjects—such as money, sex, the children, an affair, etc.—may cause the interaction to spiral downward each time. As a result, these subjects are usually never brought up except in the heat of an argument, so that they then become associated with even more hurt feelings and negative emotions.

The hurt from either an all-out argument or simply feeling shut down builds walls in your relationship that separate you and your beloved. Walls of separation erode your personal connection, which then creates a downward cycle of more misunderstanding, negativity, and disconnection. If you recognize this pattern in your own relationship, do not despair; this is very common in long-term relationships, and recognizing the pattern is the first step to changing it, starting with how you communicate!

HEART WORK: *Hearing without Ego*

As a couple, you must set aside time for sharing and understanding when you are feeling calm and open. You must both enter into a space and attitude of desiring only to understand how your beloved feels. Do not allow yourself to focus on yourself, your desires, your fears or your interpretations in this moment. As you listen to your beloved, reflect back what you are hearing until they say they feel that you truly understand.

Whether or not you see things the same way, feel the same way or understand their point of view, express your love and appreciation for your beloved and acknowledge them. When they feel heard, appreciated, and validated, then you have the groundwork for sharing different perspectives and engaging in creative problem-solving where it is needed. Love is selfless. Love is giving. Love is accepting with your whole heart. Focus on these thoughts for support and guidance as you enter into communication about your difficult issues.

IDEAS AND PRACTICES

See below for how to do the Pillow-Talk Exercise, an active-listening practice that can provide structure to help you to implement the communication ideas discussed above.

PILLOW-TALK EXERCISE

This exercise should be done two nights in a row. The first night, one of you will be the listener. The listener will ask the questions (sample questions below) and then do nothing but listen—no interrupting, correcting, judging, eye-rolls, sighs, or gestures. The listener is coming to this exercise with an open heart and a single desire to hear, understand, and acknowledge their beloved.

The person answering the questions should do their best to give full and complete answers. Go deep into your heart, and open yourself up to your beloved. This work is so important! On the second night, the roles should be switched. Here are a few prompts to guide the conversation:

- What is your favorite thing about being married to me?
- What is your deepest desire for us?
- Where/how do you like me to touch you sexually?
- Are you satisfied with our sexual connection?
- What are your dreams for us?

Talking stick

The tradition of a talking stick comes from native cultures, where a stick would be passed during councils and only the person holding the stick would be allowed to speak. You can use a talking stick with your beloved when you are communicating about important subjects. Agree that the person holding the stick is the only person who may talk, and the other person is reminded to place their full attention on the beloved, open their heart, and listen deeply. Then the stick can be passed. This is also a great practice to use with children; you can even create one together as a couple or a family.

pairings

- Lavender essential oil. The scent of lavender can support conversations with your beloved by calming your anxieties and fears and giving you a sense of peace that supports openness to sharing your heart and hearing clearly. Use a diffuser to fill your space with the scent, or put a few drops on your wrist and heart.

Journal on Pillow Talk

Use this space to journal about how your
communication with your beloved has
been, and how it felt to do the Pillow-Talk
Exercise.

_____

_____

_____

_____

_____

_____

_____

_____

_____

_____

_____

_____

_____

_____

_____

_____

_____

Healing Wounds

releasing the past

Eventually you will come to
understand that love heals
everything, and love is all there is.

~GARY ZUKAV

Everyone carries wounds and scars from past experiences. Whether they come from this relationship, other relationships, your childhood, or even past lives, these wounds still affect you today. They come from being neglected or abused when you needed to be loved. They come from life events or circumstances that were so different from how you "knew" your life should be that your resistance caused a tear in the fabric of your soul.

Like the wind, these wounds are invisible, but their effects are seen. They lie under the surface, and anytime a person, relationship, or circumstance reminds you of the wound, it flares up and causes you to react as if you were in the midst of the pain all over again. Without healing these wounds, you cannot fully experience the present; you cannot enter into deep and authentic relationship with another person; and you cannot achieve the self-mastery to ultimately live in peace, love, and happiness.

YOURSELF

Most wounds are caused by our own resistance. When you process an unpleasant experience and find meaning and even benefit in it, they are no longer wounds. For example, perhaps you are considering leaving your job to pursue another opportunity. The new opportunity is exciting and very appealing, but you are concerned about the uncertainty of change and of the apparent stability and safety of your current position. Then you are surprised to receive a notice that your company is downsizing and you are being laid off. If you view this situation as a gift, a sign from the universe that you should take advantage of the other opportunity, then you will not create an emotional wound from the unpleasant experience of being laid off.

However, if you view the layoff as an indictment of your competence, as a sign of rejection from your current company, or as something that takes away your choice of staying where you are, then you create resistance, resentment, and fear that cause an energetic wound in your psyche and emotional body. So the same event can either create an emotional wound or not, and can continue to live as negativity inside of you, to be experienced over and over again—or not. It is your own choice of which story you tell yourself about your life experiences that determine which way it goes.

A first step to healing old wounds is to look back on where they originated, and to give them the proper meaning. Everything that happens in life is a gift. There are no such things as coincidences, bad luck, or accidents. Everything is an opportunity that can be used to learn and grow. You are always exactly where you need to be on your path, in the perfect place at the perfect time. Your ability to accept this premise—to remember this fact and know its truth even in the midst of a busy life—is your key to healing old wounds and preventing new hurts from being created inside yourself.

THE COUPLE

Deep emotional wounds act as a barrier between you and your beloved. Sometimes one of you has an especially strong emotional reaction that is out of balance with the situation for no apparent reason. Other times, a past hurt can color the way you look at and feel about your beloved in the present. One or both of you may build strong defensive shells around your heart, designed to protect you from hurt but actually obstructing deep connection. Regardless of how this pain presents itself, the gift of your relationship is that you and your beloved can help heal each other.

Remember that you and your beloved are not together by accident; you each bring medicine that the other needs. Your love is the key to healing. As each of you heals, you will be even better able to share your love and accelerate each other's healing. This creates a virtuous cycle of love and healing that not only uplifts each of you as individuals but enlightens your relationship toward new heights of connection and inspiration.

HEART WORK: *Unconditional Love*

The heart work for healing emotional wounds is *trust and love.* Trust in the divine plan, and love your beloved unconditionally. Trusting the divine plan is to see the gift in everything that happens in your life, or to at least believe that there is a gift for you in everything that happens. As mentioned above, this practice will reframe how you see your past hurts; this will support their healing, and allow you to prevent potential present and future wounds before they can cause you pain and interfere in your life.

Loving unconditionally in this context means to see past whatever negativity your beloved might direct toward you. Anytime that your beloved expresses anger, attack, or negativity of any kind, it is because of pain. The greatest gift that you can give is to refrain from reacting in kind, and instead to simply *be* love. Ultimately, what you want is to stop the expression of negativity toward you—and the only way for that to happen is for you to help heal whatever wound is causing their pain, fear, and anxiety in that moment.

It takes practice, strength, and a high level of consciousness to learn not to take negativity personally and to respond in loving kindness. Speak only empathetic words; gently inquire into the feelings behind the negativity, and shower the wounds with love, care, acknowledgment, and compassion. This is the path to healing for both of you, and the path to your own Sacred Relationship.

IDEAS AND PRACTICES

See below for an exercise to help you begin to heal wounding events in your life by changing the stories you are telling yourself about them.

CHANGE-THE-STORY EXERCISE

In this exercise you will examine wounding events in your life, and then take away their power over you with the following steps:

- Make a list of negative, disastrous, or wounding events in your life.

- Choose one of these events, and sit with a pen and journal in a quiet area where you won't be interrupted.

- Consider your soul/spirit sitting in Heaven, before you were born, planning out your life. If you planned this wounding event for yourself as a gift, what would that gift be? What gift of learning or insight, or what new opportunity or experience, did you receive? Write down your thoughts and feelings.

- Focus on the gifts that you received from this event, and let the pain that was caused by your resistance, and the fear that was caused by the change and the unknown at the time, melt away. Stay in a deeply relaxed and contemplative state as the feelings of gratitude grow in your chest and spread throughout your body.

- Think of any people who were involved in this hurt—people you may view as hurting you or being the cause of your pain and suffering. Journal your feelings about these people.

- After finishing, take the same feelings of gratitude and direct them toward these people. Be grateful that they agreed to take on the role in your life that gave you these lessons or gifts. See these people as divine teachers who only acted in this way as a gift to you. Stay with these thoughts until you are able to feel a deep, loving gratitude for both the events and the people that led to this wound. The vibration of gratitude will perform deep healing for you.

Take time each day to perform the same exercise for each wounding event on your list, generating feelings of gratitude and appreciation for the circumstances and people who helped lead to your growth and evolution as a person.

Energy healing

Consider visiting an energy healer for the release and healing of negative energies that live in your body from old hurts and wounds. Reiki practitioners or shamanic healers, for instance, can work with energy to help heal and release energetic barriers and wounds from past hurts, even if they do not register in your conscious mind.

pairings

- Book: *Disappearance of the Universe: Straight Talk about Illusions, Past Lives, Religion, Sex, Politics, and the Miracles of Forgiveness* by Gary Renard. This book is a great introduction to the teachings of *A Course in Miracles* and to using forgiveness as a path to healing.

- Song: "Mahalo" by Mary Isis. *Mahalo* is the Hawaiian word for "thank you." This is a wonderful, soothing song that puts you in the energetic vibration of gratitude for everything that has happened in your life and for the gifts that everything has brought to you.

Journal on Healing Wounds

Use this space to journal about your past hurts, as you recognize with gratitude the gifts that you received from these events.

_____

_____

_____

_____

_____

_____

_____

_____

_____

_____

_____

_____

_____

_____

_____

_____

_____

_____

Trust

trust is the opposite of fear

[This] is what we must learn
in this age: . . . to live out of
pure trust, without any security
in existence—trust in the ever-
present help of the spiritual
world. Truly, nothing else will
do if our courage is not to fail us.

~RUDOLF STEINER

One of the concepts that we revisit throughout this book is that the creation of a Sacred Relationship requires us to raise our point of view to a much higher perspective. While most of us mainly see and feel the immediate physical and material aspects of our lives, true peace, joy, and love can only come when we look at the bigger picture and true meaning of life, trusting that, in the bigger scheme, we are taken care of, and everything we experience is for our highest good and best interest.

At the Sacred Relationship live retreats, we start the opening circle with a talk on "trusting the process" that is about to unfold over the next few days, as couples who join us often feel resistance to the work in the beginning. By the end of the last day, though, all of the couples have gotten a small taste of how trusting and not rushing the universal plan can have a truly sweet reward.

YOURSELF

Wherever you are in your life, whatever your circumstance, no matter what is happening to you right now, the universe has perfectly conspired to put you smack-dab in the middle of your destiny. The key is to understand that the purpose of your life here on Earth is to learn and grow in the realization that you are a divine being consisting only of pure love.

The more you grow in this way, the more joy, peace, and love you feel in every moment of every day. Moreover, you are not alone on this journey; you have teachers and spiritual guides whose only desire is to help and support you.

An attendee at one of the Sacred Living Movement Brotherhood retreats had a rather intense experience during an afternoon visioning exercise in the woods. He was sitting under a tree meditating when suddenly he sensed danger. He saw a man and a dog approaching; the man began yelling at him, and the dog charged at him as if to attack. Our friend then took off running at top speed, and jumped over a creek to escape the dog. Then he wandered in the woods until he found a fire road, where he was able to get cell-phone reception and contact us to pick him up.

The next day, when we did a meditation to connect to our spirit guides, he was shown that all along the way his guides were helping and protecting him. They aroused him to the impending danger, he felt as if they held him by his arms and carried him as he outran the dog and jumped over a creek, and they guided him through the woods to safety. This was a very powerful teaching for him, and an example that even in seemingly difficult times our guides are with us.

When you are able to trust the perfection of where you are and what you are experiencing, then all resistance to your life situation dissolves. Without resistance there cannot be suffering, stress, anger, or frustration. A deep sense of trust assures you that what is happening now—and what is to come—are all part of a universal plan aimed to bring you peace, joy, and happiness.

THE COUPLE

The key to a Sacred Relationship is to be able to give nothing but love to your beloved, regardless of the situation. This is difficult when you are angry or frustrated with your partner because they are doing something that you don't want them to do, or not doing something that you think they should. Total and complete trust is the antidote to this toxic cocktail, and can leave you feeling heard, loved, and cared for.

In every situation, train yourself to remember that whatever your beloved is doing is what they need for their own growth path, and however it affects you is just what you need to practice for your own growth. *It is especially helpful, when you are having difficulty in your relationship, to view the actions of your beloved not as their own but as your spirit guides working through them to offer you what you need to practice and work on.* The trust that what you each experience is coming from a higher wisdom, and is a gift—regardless of how much resistance you may feel toward it—will allow you to be loving and generous with your beloved.

HEART WORK: *Be Open to the Higher Purpose*

The first step in allowing trust to rule your mind is to open to the fact that you may not always know what is best for yourself in the long run. When you are less conscious, your actions and reactions are ruled by simple pleasure-seeking and pain-avoidance. Human beings tend to want to stay in their comfort zones, and will fight to avoid rocking the boat. However, you need to move through areas of discomfort to reach new levels of thinking and being that will bring greater rewards than you can possibly imagine from your current point of view.

For example, maybe you need to experience the pain of an affair or other betrayal in your relationship to eradicate the fear of loss, or to learn how to give the grace of forgiveness. Maybe you need to make mistakes that hurt your beloved so that you can learn to break destructive habits, grow in humility, and awaken to the true value of your love. Everything that happens is truly a gift. But in order to receive the benefit of the gift, you must drop your resistance, trust that it is given to you in love, and be open to what is being offered.

IDEAS AND PRACTICES

Finding the gift

Create a new practice for yourself to shift your perspective when you experience difficulties. Every time you run into what seems like a challenge or an unpleasant or even traumatic experience, take a minute to remind yourself that there is a gift in everything, and discover what valuable teaching you can take from it. It could be anything—learning patience, reducing attachment to material things, or seeing situations from another person's perspective.

Finding the gift in all things may be challenging at first, but it is a habit that will change your life. For example, whenever we are in traffic, we choose to see it as a gift—that perhaps we are being protected from an accident or other unpleasantries.

GUIDED WRITING

If you are struggling with an especially difficult situation, you can call upon your spirit guides for help in understanding it.

- Take some time in a quiet place with a pen and journal. Begin with a short meditation, focusing on being present and in a relaxed and calm state of mind. Then open yourself to your spirit guides, and ask to connect with them.

- When you feel ready, open your journal and pick up your pen, and write a question to your spirit guides, such as, "What is the purpose of this situation in my life?" or "What good can I take from this situation?" or "What am I meant to learn from this?" Then write whatever comes into your mind. Do not edit or judge; just write in a free-flowing manner.

- You can then ask follow-up questions and ask for answers.

- When you are finished, re-read everything that you have written, and look for insights into your current situation.

PAIRINGS

- Card deck: *Trust Your Vibes Oracle Cards: A Powerful Tool Kit for Awakening Your Sixth Sense* by Sonia Choquette. Oracle decks can assist you in an awakening phase of your life. Pick one card every morning, read its meaning, and light a candle as a reminder to lean into trust throughout your day.

- Auric cleanser: "Trust the Universal Plan Auric Cleanser" by Soul Tree Essences. This is a spray that you can use to aurically cleanse yourself after a shower, or just use throughout the day to lift you out of the mundane and keep those trusting vibes floating around you!

Journal on Trust

Use this space to journal about past and current difficulties, and the benefits and growth that you have received from them.

_____

_____

_____

_____

_____

_____

_____

_____

_____

_____

_____

_____

_____

_____

_____

_____

_____

Love's Nectar

it's all the gold

Life is a flower, of which
love is the honey.

~VICTOR HUGO

Love is alive in us from our first breath. It is the sustenance of all life; it is the one thing we seek out more than any other. When we fall in love, it's as if the heavens opened up and God smiled upon us, with all the gold laid at our feet. We are rich with joy, have abundant, free-flowing energy, and somehow harness a love superpower that makes us believe we are capable of anything. A miracle lands on us, and all of a sudden the sky is more blue, food is more delicious, and giggles tickle our lips as we daydream about each other. For perhaps the first time, we are awake to life and all its beauty and magic and, like a curious child, we want more and more and more. We seal it with a kiss, and guzzle the nectar as if it were blessed water from the sacred springs of the gods.

So what happens to all these ooey and gooey feelings? Why are we not always sticky with love's magic honey? Time happens; we settle in with each other and embrace the mundane, forgetting how awake we once were. We need to gently arise from our stagnant slumbers to wrap each other in a new love—an intentional love.

YOURSELF

The beginnings of love's nectar in your life can often lead you off the path of "me" and onto the path of "us," which is what you want—sort of. It's important to be invested in the "us" after you fall in love, but not to the exclusion of who you are—your dreams, your visions, and your own spiritual growth. In fact, the nature of true love uplifts individual aspirations, holds space for them to grow, and encourages their flight into the world. Coercive or controlling expressions of love do the opposite. Staying in Divine Mind will help you strike a nice balance between self and other, and encourage right relationship with your destiny.

THE COUPLE

Intentional love serves you both. It says, "I choose you with consciousness and a splash of mindfulness—today, tomorrow, and every day." Intentional love is where the heart work lives, because you have been reacquainted with your desire to live out a sacred experience with your beloved. This is huge—so many couples split up because they get bored with each other, the passion dies, and they forget why they came together in the first place.

We live in a society dominated by pop culture and celebrities in regularly rotating relationships. Immediate gratification rules the day, and relationships become an exchangeable currency. When we understand soul contracts, intentional love, and living in high vibration, however, we seek a new level of perfection, and we define relationships with mindful awareness. We do the heart work to unfold the deepest layers of ourselves to the other, and thus experience the truest thing in life there is—Sacred Love.

HEART WORK: *Morning Gratitude Prayers*

Gratitude is a superpower, and it is the most important ingredient in the cauldron of manifestation. Start each day with gratitude for the other and for the universe that supports you. Stand in front of your beloved, hold hands, and say what you are grateful for. If weather allows, step outside, bare feet grounded on Mother Earth and hands up to the sky, and be grateful for every single thing you have and all the lessons you have been given. You can play a song like "Mahalo" by Mary Isis when you do this gratitude practice, as it amplifies your intention with beauty. And if you can lend your voice to the music, it will help the heavens hear your joy.

IDEAS AND PRACTICES

Love journal

Buy a beautiful journal that you and your beloved can share. Keep it in the Sacred Space you created, and use it as a touchstone for romance, insights, and daydreams. Each of you takes turns writing in the journal, starting each entry with "Dear (fill in the other's name), . . ." and then write a little love letter. This regular practice will keep the intentions flowing freely, and keep the dreaming fresh with perspective and invigorated with consciousness.

SPIRIT LOVE INCENSE

Renew your connection to each other with this sensual scent.

- 3 parts sandalwood, ground
- 2 parts copal resin, ground
- 1 part vanilla bean, ground
- 10 drops rose essential oil

Grind everything into a powder.

Light an incense charcoal and, once it's hot all the way through, pour a little of the incense powder on top.

You can also substitute essential oils for the plant materials, and make a blend to use in an oil burner.

LOVE'S NECTAR POTION

Take this potion daily for a month to raise your vibration and support your sacred unfolding.

- ½ cup organic wild roses, dried
- ½ cup raw cacao nibs
- 1 cinnamon stick
- 1 tablespoon ginger, dried
- 2 cups raw honey from beloved bees
- 3 drops rose or orchid flower essence

Pour honey into a heatproof bowl over a pot of gently simmering water. You don't want to boil the honey, just to warm it up.

Keeping your heat low and gentle, add the roses, cacao nibs, and spices to the warm honey, and stir well to combine thoroughly.

Remove bowl from heat, and let your honey infuse for 1–6 hours. The longer it sits, the stronger it will be.

Add flower essences.

Strain honey through a fine-mesh strainer over a large bowl, or directly into jars. Place on your Sacred Relationship Altar, and let infuse for another week.

Take this elixir once a day over the next month.

pairings

- Song: "Path of Transformation" by Mary Isis. This song has an ability to bring you right into your divine selves, and can serve as a daily reminder of your transforming, intentional love—to the level of the Sacred.

- Book: *True Love: A Practice for Awakening the Heart* by Thich Nhat Hanh. A lovely book by a Zen Buddhist monk about the tender place love lives, and the nature of real love. This is a favorite—if you pick up any book on love, this should be it!

Journal on Love's Nectar

Journal your feelings on the sweet beginnings of your relationship and your recharged commitment to intentional loving of the other.

_____

_____

_____

_____

_____

_____

_____

_____

_____

_____

_____

_____

_____

_____

_____

_____

SECTION TWO

WE

Practice

LOVE IS MIND-PATIENCE

Sustained love takes heart work!

It does not rest beneath the cloak of disillusion. It looks the dragon in the eyes. It frees the chained soul, and never backs down.

Sustained love takes karuna—*compassion!*

It holds the hand of the aching heart, soothing it with words of empathy and care.

Sustained love takes fierce will and dedication!

It is not easily shaken with wild whims of dissent, but stays true and bold.

Sustained love takes surrender!

It trusts enough to reveal tender moments and welcome soft vulnerabilities.

Sustained love takes Divine Mind!

It is ever-patient, and lives in conscious awareness, stirring the cauldron of hope and high vibrations.

Sustained love takes two people!

It is the only course on which to set sail—if the two adventurers are ready, willing, and able to travel uncharted territory toward their own personal island of bliss.

Love Warrior

love with courage, strength, and resolve

It is better to live one day as a lion
than a thousand days as a lamb.

~ROMAN PROVERB

Being a warrior means dedicating yourself to accomplishing your mission. Living as a love warrior requires training your body, mind, and will to being only love, and expressing only love.

YOURSELF

Being in love is your natural state; however, virtually all of us have forgotten this truth. We have developed habits that keep us living in fear, frustration, sadness, disappointment, and resentment. Leaving these habits behind and allowing ourselves to return to pure love is the key to our happiness and fulfillment as individuals, and to the blossoming of our relationships.

The samurai is one of the greatest and most famous of warrior cultures. Key aspects of the samurai philosophy, known as *bushido*, were discipline and mastery. The samurai focused their lives on the mastery of their military skills. This involved practicing not only archery, swordsmanship, or other military arts every day, but also art, poetry, and meditation to calm and center the mind. The samurai recognized that for true greatness one must dedicate one's entire being to the craft.

The pursuit of a Sacred Relationship requires you to become a warrior for love. There will be times when your habitual life will tempt you to express yourself in anger, hurt, or frustration, based on your current beliefs about when it is justified to belittle, yell, or withdraw your love and attention. So your warrior spirit must be constantly vigilant and dedicated to love.

Like the samurai, engage your entire being in this pursuit. Perfection is not easily attained, so when you find yourself thinking or acting in nonloving ways, that is when you must reach down deep to find your warrior spirit, and the courage and strength to step out of anger into love.

THE COUPLE

Love expressed between you and your beloved is the entire story of a Sacred Relationship. When you are in love, acting from love, and expressing love, then you grow and strengthen your relationship. Anything else will wither and weaken your connection. Being love warriors for each other means that each of you makes the decision and commitment to give and express only love. Therefore, you need to stay vigilant—pay attention to what you are feeling and expressing, and do not accept anything less than love. You will need the strength and courage of the warrior to live up to this vow.

Whenever you express something other than love, your ego is the culprit. Whether you are frustrated because you believe things should be different, or believe that you deserve more, or that you have been disrespected, the root of it all is ego. It is also ego that makes it difficult for you to step back, admit that you are not fulfilling your commitment of unconditional love, and make a different choice.

We have so deeply tied our sense of self-worth to being right that it truly takes the dedication, strength, and persistence of the warrior to make the shift to identifying with love instead. Your beloved is your greatest teacher in this regard. Look to your beloved to see your reflection, so that you can clearly see where you are expressing love and where you are not. In addition, use any occasion when they are not expressing love as a training for you to express love even in the face of difficulty.

Mastery and perfection do not come easily or immediately, but the opportunities to begin practicing are being presented to you in every moment. Be a warrior for your beloved, be a warrior for yourself, and you will reap the rewards and uncover the treasure.

HEART WORK: *Choose to Be Love*

A theme that we revisit many times in this book is that true love is unconditional; it is a gift that you offer to your beloved without asking or requiring anything in return. True love is not transactional—it is a pure giveaway. You must train your mind to let go of your habits of anger, attachment, selfishness, or any other thought patterns that lead to negative words or actions toward your beloved. This mind training is simply based on telling yourself different stories about your life experiences and replacing the negative thoughts with positive ones.

However, changing these habits requires the strength to let go of the ego, so that you can recognize when you are acting in a counterproductive way. It also requires the courage and will to make a different choice—over and over again. The strength, persistence, and unrelenting desire to walk this path are the warrior qualities that will make the difference between continuing in your possibly destructive current patterns and enjoying the pleasure and gratification of a Sacred Relationship.

IDEAS AND PRACTICES

A Course in Miracles workbook

A Course in Miracles (ACIM) describes an entire thought system, including exercises that train your mind to see everything in love and forgiveness. This is an intense and transformative journey, so I suggest you start with *The Disappearance of the Universe* by Gary Renard as a wonderful, accessible introduction to ACIM. The ACIM workbook itself is a year of daily practices that can help you to become a love warrior.

PAIRINGS

- Book/Movie: *Way of the Peaceful Warrior* by Dan Millman. This is an inspirational semiautobiographical tale of the trials of spiritual growth and the rewards that can be obtained by taking the warrior path to overcome all obstacles.

Journal on Love Warrior

Use this space to journal about times and circumstances where you could have been a stronger love warrior in your relationship. Identify what you want to improve, and make a plan for how to recognize these situations in the moment they occur—and for how you will respond differently in the future.

It's All About the Energy

*the quality of your energy determines
the quality of your relationship*

Everything is energy, and that's all
there is to it. Match the frequency
of the reality you want, and you
cannot help but get that reality. It
can be no other way. This is physics.

~BASHAR

This week we introduce energy—a very simple but powerful concept that will be the foundation of the work going forward.

One thing upon which modern physics and ancient spiritual traditions agree is that everything is energy. The reason that we perceive differences among material objects, feelings, thoughts, and emotions is that they are all still energy, but vibrating at different frequencies. So the difference between feeling happiness and sadness is just the frequency of vibration that you hold in that particular moment.

We want to help you learn to be aware of the quality of energy that you are in, so that you can then choose the level of vibration that matches the experience of life that you want.

YOURSELF

Tuning your energy to feel good is like adjusting the frequency on your car radio to get to the station that you want to listen to. If you tune in to anger, then you will get anger; if you tune into joy, you will get joy. The challenge for many of us is that we are used to letting outside events and influences control who we are and how we feel. If something happens the way we think it should, our vibration rises and we feel happy. If something creates challenge or difficulty, then the frequency drops and we feel frustrated and unhappy.

The reality, however, is that we can consciously control the frequency of our own vibration by choosing to regularly raise our energy, improve our attitude, and live in awareness in the present moment, no matter what is happening externally. We only need to be awake to our personal energy, and intentionally do everything we can to take deep drinks of good vibes, joy, and love.

Learning to control your own vibration means retraining your mind. Any habits determining where your energy goes in stressful or difficult situations were learned or created by you. Therefore, they are in your control, and you can choose differently at any time. Pay close attention to the stories that you tell yourself, and then shift them to bring yourself to a higher vibration.

For example, if your beloved is angry, critical or attacking you, stay in high vibration and see that they are just acting out of their own pain. Bring yourself to the high vibration of compassion, and look to understand and heal rather than lowering your vibration to defensiveness and counterattack.

THE COUPLE

The quality of energy that you hold within yourself extends to connections with others. A relationship between two people can be thought of as a pot containing all of the energies that each person has directed toward the other throughout their entire relationship. This includes every word spoken between them, every action taken, and even every thought that they have had about each other. The quality of your relationship as it stands now is the net result of the vibrations of all of those energies mixed together.

So if you want to raise the quality of your love, your relationship soup needs to be filled with only ingredients of love, joy, peace, and splashes of as many positive energies as you can conjure up. Serve this up with a side of radical purity and divine intentions, and you will be consuming the very best love tonic on the planet!

To make a drastic shift in your relationship, it is best to completely dump out all of the old energies through intense release work, and then start over with an empty pot. However, you can only mix in the energy vibrations that are alive in you at the present moment. You can't mix in love if you feel anger, and you can't mix in anger if you feel love. So, to express love toward your beloved, you yourself must be a living expression of love. Up your vibe soup! Only add in the good stuff, and your hearts and souls will forever be nourished.

HEART WORK: Changing the Stories

The work of raising the vibration of your relationship begins with the stories you tell yourself about the connection you share with your beloved. We offer many different ideas, techniques, and exercises to elevate your stories to a sacred level—but it is critical that you pay close attention to the dialogue in your head, and make positive shifts anywhere you find negativity.

Every time you perform a loving act, offer a kind, healing word, or have a positive thought toward your beloved, you not only raise the energy of your relationship but catapult your own spiritual connection and mastery to a higher level. Similarly, whenever you take steps to raise your own personal vibration, you are then in a position to effortlessly and naturally express high-vibration energy toward your beloved.

This is a self-reinforcing cycle, because the more positivity you express to your beloved, the better they will feel, and then naturally return loving gestures to you, which will make you feel better and want to express love back, and so on. This spiraling up is desirable; it is the opposite of the downward spiral that you experience any time you get into an argument where insults and accusations are exchanged. Focus on your own awareness, and consciously choose high vibrations as the path to joy and happiness in your own life— and see the positive results on all the relationships around you.

IDEAS AND PRACTICES

Energy clearing

Negative, low-vibration energies tend to build up in our bodies over a lifetime. There are many ways to clear these out so that they don't affect you, such as visiting a shaman, Reiki practitioner, or other energy worker. This type of "energetic cleansing" can be a powerful catalyst for positive change.

Vibe-ups

"Vibe-ups" are practices that will raise your vibration at times when you are feeling low, frustrated, anxious, or angry. There are many different ideas and exercises to choose from, so find the ones that work well for you. Here are a few of our favorites:

- **Crystal water.** Keep a water bottle with you all the time, to stay hydrated. We always put a crystal in our water bottle so that the energy of the crystal infuses into the water, which then is passed on to us when we drink it. You can use rose quartz for love, clear quartz for clarity, etc.

- **Aromatherapy.** Many folks are uplifted by the smells of essential oils. Try a variety of them to find which ones appeal to you.

- **White sage.** Buy a sage bundle at your local metaphysical store or online. Light the dried leaves, and then blow out the flame and waft the smoke to bathe yourself. This is a common Native American practice for cleansing and purifying negative energies, as the smoke of plant materials such as sage leaf and palo santo wood are known to do this. It can also be helpful to call upon your spirit guides to help raise your vibration while you are doing this cleansing.

- **Gratitude.** Any time you find yourself resisting something, be in deep gratitude for the ability to be able to do it: "I am grateful to have two arms that work to wash these dishes." "I am grateful to have the strength to move this box." Gratitude is a high-vibration feeling, and being in gratitude will lift your vibration immediately.

- You can find additional vibe-up practices in the book *Practicing Happy: A Spiritual Workout for Happiness and Fulfillment in Your Life* by Tim Daulter.

Personal release work

Doing your own release work is a self-help method for eliminating negative vibrational energies that hold you back from opening up to higher vibrations in your life and relationship. One way to do this is to write down your emotions, thoughts, or unhealed hurts on a piece of paper and then burn the paper in a fire. As the paper is consumed, hold the intention that the energy it describes is also being released from you at the same time.

Personal and relationship practices

We will go deeper into practices that can elevate your relationship in other parts of this book, but it is critically important to create daily practices that raise your own personal vibration and send high-vibration energy to your beloved, raising the sacredness of your relationship. View these practices as a physical fitness practice, in that they aren't effective if only practiced once, or once in awhile, but only if they are constantly reinforced and maintained.

pairings

- Book: *Practicing Happy* by Tim Daulter. This book offers an in-depth look at shifting your internal stories and raising your personal vibration, plus practices in the form of a spiritual workout to provide structure along this path.
- Crystals: a variety of crystals will absorb and block low-vibration energy, including amethyst, citrine, clear quartz, and rose quartz. Explore in a crystal store to find descriptions of many stones, and choose one that feels good to you to wear, carry, or keep where you spend a great deal of time. Taking a shower and/or soaking in an Epsom-salt bath are also good ways of removing low-vibration energies.

Journal on It's All About the Energy

Use this space to journal about the people, habits, and thoughts that bring low-vibration energies into your life—and about ways to replace them with those that will raise your vibration.

_____

_____

_____

_____

_____

_____

_____

_____

_____

_____

_____

_____

_____

_____

_____

_____

_____

_____

_____

Divine Mind

live by spiritual clarity and pure thoughts

No thoughts go unheard.

~ANONYMOUS

Our thoughts make up the inner landscape of our creative mind, our rational world, our humor, our private ideas, and all that encompasses our uniqueness. The quote above speaks to the fact that all of our thoughts get translated into energy that is then sent out into the universe and to those around us. That means all the positive and negative stuff gets cast out into the universe, millions of times a day, and you alone are responsible for your part in that casting.

Practicing Divine Mind means that not only are you living in mindful awareness, you are actively choosing to send more positivity and high-vibration thoughts into the world. This in turn creates a more peaceful inner landscape for you. This practice is a masterful objective, as it also shapes your consciousness in a new way, and gifts you with the skill to respond to situations from love and compassion rather than taking an immediate reactive stance to whatever comes up.

YOURSELF

Are you in control of your thoughts, or do they spin out of control into places of anxiety, fear, stress, and anger? If you believe you are not in control of your thoughts, you must start practicing Divine Mind; and if you believe you are in control of them, you must also start practicing Divine Mind, for we are always students. Find the personal discipline you may need to take up a daily meditation, and unfold the reverent side of who you are.

THE COUPLE

Divine Mind comes from the greater good, not from individual need. This is key to understanding the concept. If we come from a place of individual need rather than collective consciousness, we react based on thinking solely of ourselves in the moment, and this limits our potential to grow as human beings. People will offend us; they will say negative things to or about us; they will say things we massively disagree with; they will do crappy things that hurt us—but

Divine-Mind response is to look for ways to love them, and see the teachings in the situation, and find the gold rather than react to the offenses. BE DIVINE.

When we choose Divine Mind, we elevate both ourselves and humanity. Each divine response changes the world a little bit. This concept is important in your relationship with your beloved, because when you approach each other with Divine Mind, you are open rather than closed, awake rather than asleep, wanting and willing rather than resisting. This is how you will tap into your intuition and elevate your spirit self to walk your heart path in humility and peace-full awareness with each other.

HEART WORK: *It's a Gift*

Divine Mind is an elevated way to respond to everything. It's a gift you can give yourself every day. It's choosing to respond with spiritual clarity and love rather than anger, fear, frustration, or hurt; it's a purely high-vibe response. Each time something happens to you that you perceive as negative, train yourself to say, "How can I respond in Divine Mind?" When you can take any issue that you think of as negative and say, "How can I respond in love, compassion, and high vibration?"—*that is Divine Mind.*

IDEAS AND PRACTICES

Meditation

There are so many forms of meditation—from sitting to walking to washing the dishes—and each one brings you to Divine Mind if done with conscious intention and joy. In Buddhism, mundane tasks can be elevated to sacredness, and when this is accomplished you become the master of your own mind, able to experience living in full presence and awareness. This is a master calling; the elevated mind knows only freedom, and if you live there you can have beauty and peace in all of your relationships.

Spend at least ten to fifteen minutes a day in your choice of meditation, be it sitting in your Sacred Space and lighting a candle and getting centered, doing a walking meditation in nature, having still moments with high-vibration music while trying to empty your mind, or any other form you can think of. A famous Buddhist quote is, "If you think you cannot meditate for ten minutes a day, meditate for an hour a day."

WASHING DISHES MEDITATION

Bring presence to your daily routine, and elevate the mundane to the Sacred. When you wash dishes, bring joy to the task with love from your heart. Wash each dish with care and consciousness, as if you were washing Baby Buddha. This level of presence shifts that task, bringing your thoughts to Divine Mind, radiating positive energy into your home, and uplifting those around you.

pairings

- Song: "Cosmic Bliss" by Mary Isis. This song is great to use when meditating, washing the dishes, or practicing Divine Mind in your home. It also shifts the energy in your home to create a more sacred environment.

- Crown-chakra elevation: use the essential oil of frankincense as a quick anointing oil for your crown chakra; a little dab on your third eye will also help you stay in Divine Mind. This is particularly helpful in the beginning, when you are practicing presence and elevating your thoughts on a daily basis. Frankincense helps you connect to your higher spiritual self, which is particularly useful before your meditation practice.

Journal on Divine Mind

Use this space to reflect on how you use
Divine Mind in your daily interactions
with others.

_____

_____

_____

_____

_____

_____

_____

_____

_____

_____

_____

_____

_____

_____

_____

_____

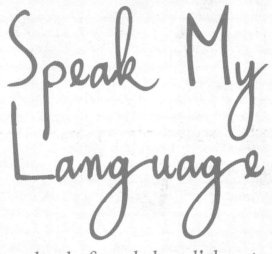

Speak My Language

school of our beloved's heart

Sometimes the smallest things take up the most room in your heart.

~WINNIE THE POOH

We love in the way that we want to be loved. So much can be understood about relationships with just that simple sentence. We typically give the way we want our beloveds to give to us, and if they don't meet our expectations and reciprocate, our feelings get hurt because we interpret this as not caring. In reality, however, they truly may not know how to meet our needs, or the various ways to express their feelings that would truly speak to our hearts. We all need a class at the school of our beloveds' hearts—and we need to study up good, so we can truly learn what lights their fires!

YOURSELF

Have you ever taken the time to sit and meditate on what truly brings you joy in your relationship? Do you know the specific things that stir the romance cauldron of your heart? It's important for you to take the time to look deeply into these answers in order to really claim your own truths about the give-and-take of love. And if you are seeking to be compassionate with your beloved, it's equally important to offer yourself such grace and wisdom. This is good for both you and your connection!

THE COUPLE

If you seek to serve your relationship in the highest vibrations, take time to really learn how your beloved wants to be cared for. What truly turns them on and makes them happy? Studying each other's hearts is a noble cause, worth undertaking. The only way to true happiness is through love and compassion. The Sanskrit word for compassion is *karuna,* and it is one of the pillars of true love.

Think about speaking the words, "I love you" to your beloved— "you" being the key word. If a true heart speaks such a proclamation, it seeks to also understand and accept who that person is and what relieves their suffering. One kind word, one thoughtful gesture, or one act of service can literally change someone's world. Acts of kindness bring forth the best in each other, and are the foundation of any love relationship. Seeking to love your partner in a way they want you to says that you are willing to live from this space of selfless karuna.

HEART WORK: *Five Love Languages Based on the Work of Dr. Gary Chapman*

There are "five love languages," based on the well-received book of that name by Dr. Gary Chapman. According to Dr. Chapman, when we can understand each other's preferences for how we like to be loved, we have a better shot at a long, healthy relationship.

Take a look at the five basic love languages below, and see which is your number-one choice of how you prefer your beloved would show love to you. Then try to determine what your beloved's choice would be. In reality, all of these ways feed the soul, but we are typically drawn to a primary love language.

We have renamed them here, but the five love languages are:

1. **Sweet Talk** (words of affirmation). You prefer that your beloved use sweet words and gratitude affirmations as a way to express love for you. It is important for you to hear and know that you are appreciated, valued, and still sexy as hell!

2. **Be Captivated** (quality time shared together). You want your beloved's full attention, and seek to spend quality time together sharing ideas, dreams, and interests in an engaged manner.

3. **Naked Time** (touching each other). You prefer physical touch as your primary means of love expression, whether through hand-holding, heart-hugs, kissing, affections, being naked together, or sharing sexy time.

4. **Heart Gifts** (sweet and thoughtful goodies). Thoughtful little gifts are your preferred form of being shown love. These might be just fresh-cut flowers, or a little trinket bought to show you that you were thought of during the day.

5. **Acts of Service** (favors, projects, errands, leaps of faith). You appreciate your beloved doing things for you to show they care, for example, running to the store, cleaning up the house, cooking, taking care of errands, or even bigger gestures like moving across the country with you to fulfill a dream.

IDEAS AND PRACTICES

ASK-AND-ANSWER EXERCISE

Here is an exercise for you to record in your journal. Each of you answers the following questions from your own point of view, and then from your beloved's point of view. For example, if the question is, "What is the best gift you ever received from your beloved?" then you write down the best gift you ever received, along with your prediction of how you think your beloved will answer the same question. Try it with these questions:

- What is your idea of a perfect night with your beloved?
- How many times per week would be optimal for you to make love together?
- Which of the five above is your love language?
- What is the best gift that your beloved ever gave you?
- Which would mean more to you—to have your beloved do something for you, or to have your beloved say something nice to you?

Once you have both answered these questions, compare your answers. How well did you predict each other's responses? What are your and your beloved's primary love language(s)? Note your beloved's preferred love language—and be sure to use it often!

Now that you have information about your love languages (see above with Ask-and-Answer Exercise), pick weekly practices that support each of your love languages, and make a commitment to give them both a go! For example, if your beloved's love language is naked time, implement regular massages, heart-hugs, or the actual Naked Time practice once a day for a week. See how it feels, and whether your physical connection grows. Make sure each of you has a practice that the other is willing to take up with the heart of a love warrior.

pairings

- Book: *The 5 Love Languages: The Secret to Love that Lasts* by Dr. Gary Chapman. This is a great book that looks more deeply at the five love languages he describes as critical to understanding in order for a happy relationship to thrive.

Journal on Speak My Language

Use this space to reflect on each other's love languages, and how you feel you can best meet each other in this realm.

_____

_____

_____

_____

_____

_____

_____

_____

_____

_____

_____

_____

_____

_____

_____

_____

_____

_____

_____

_____

Five Daily Practices

everyday heart work

→

Be a love warrior!

~TIM DAULTER

This week will begin the process of forming and shaping your heart work in ways that are doable, bite-sized, and can fit within the constructs of a busy daily life. Taking up these practices will be an effort of will, however, and—make no mistake about it—warrior's work. Just remember that these practices are the way to reshape your relationship with your beloved into one that feels good to you!

Forming new habits takes persistence, dedication, and a huge YES from each of you in order to make this work. Every day "right action" means that these must be taken up as a part of your daily routines, and other things may have to wait. When you start to shift the importance of your relationship to Class-1 top importance, other things in your lives will also need shifting around. Say YES to being a love warrior for each other.

YOURSELF

Ask yourselves a very important question this week: "Am I willing?" A simple "yes" won't do. This requires a serious willingness shaped with purpose, intention, and a belief in a relationship far more elevated than your current state. It's a question that begs an answer of true heart-honesty in order to execute the outcome with fierce conviction.

In the beginning of the book, you were asked to give your Sacred YES to this relationship as a first step, and now you are being asked to step into warrior spirit and take on new daily love rites that will show you the path and help you walk it with ease. Take some time to meditate on this question; each of you can then offer an answer to the other as to whether you can take up this heart work in a real way and become the love remedy you both seek.

THE COUPLE

If you both take up these daily practices with a true heart and real commitment, you will see deep changes in your connection. The love between you will flourish, and you will start to remember how to live from your heart space. This will slowly begin to replace any anger and resentments that may have built up between you over the years.

These practices have been tested by many couples from all parts of the world—and they do work, if you do them! After two weeks of doing these practices, things will shift between you, but if you start to slack off your connection will suffer. Staying on the path may be the biggest challenge you both have, but remember that, like a warrior, you must be true to your word and maintain steady action every single day.

HEART WORK: *Understanding Warrior Spirit*

To understand warrior spirit is to be willing to look closely at your will, your inner strength, and your commitment to be of service to one another. When you say "yes" to anything in your life, do you typically follow through, or do you get excited at first and then allow your commitment to wane and eventually flicker out? When you say you will do something, is your word golden and noble, or do you just say "yes" without really thinking about whether you will actually follow through?

A warrior spirit is that of truth and effect; it is both the steady bow and the fierce arrow of completion. Agreeing to do the daily practices should be taken up with your noble word and your full agreement. This means that you don't miss a day of practices, and that you do them with the passion that first stirred your heart for your beloved. Being in service to another's heart is delicate, and should be handled with care and not frivolity. Own your word the way a noble wears a crown.

IDEAS AND PRACTICES

See Five Daily Couples Practices below.

FIVE DAILY COUPLES PRACTICES

1. **Gratitude practice.** Taking up a daily gratitude practice helps strengthen your consciousness muscles, and brings real focus to understanding that the less you live from an attitude of lack, the more abundance will flow in your life. Create a "gratitude journal" where you write one thing you are grateful for in your life every day. Remember to include your beloved in your gratitude practice throughout the week.

2. **My beloved.** From this day forward, every time you address your partner, refer to him or her as your BELOVED! This is a sacred term, and reminds each of you that you are living in your higher consciousness in relation to the other.

3. **Hug and kiss.** Each and every time you enter and leave your beloved's presence, give them a hug and a kiss and say, "You are my love." This means a *real* hug and a kiss on the lips, taking the time to look into each other's eyes for a moment to remind each other your truest love is standing before you.

4. **Sing praises.** Each day, say something positive about your beloved to another person. This will bring to your awareness all of the amazing things about them, and will help you to reshape some of the stories you may have told yourself about the other person.

5. **Love notes.** Each day, leave at least one sticky note with romantic or complimentary love words in places where your beloved will find them. You can also write old-fashioned love letters to each other, but these love notes are quick and easy. Pop these up around the house for your beloved to find throughout the day. This action is a sweet gesture that helps your beloved know what you are thinking about them, and can help thaw the heart space, especially if you are not currently in the best place in your relationship.

pairings

- *Sacred Gratitude Journal* by Anni Daulter and Stephanie Green. This journal, available through the Sacred Living Movement, offers daily prompts for living in gratitude. It is beautifully designed and helps bring shape and form to your practice.

- Crystal: use aquamarine to give you extra energy to accomplish your daily practices. Said to have come from the treasure chests of mermaids, it also promises strong love to believers.

Journal on Five Daily Practices

Use this space to journal about how
your daily practices are helping your
connection.

_____

_____

_____

_____

_____

_____

_____

_____

_____

_____

_____

_____

_____

_____

_____

_____

_____

_____

Word Medicine

what we say matters

A poem begins as a
lump in the throat.

~ROBERT FROST

Much like poetry, life is filled with the deepest wells of pain, the highest highs of joy, and all the in-between wonder a human can hold. While we all wish that everything we said waxed poetic and could be filled with the highest-vibration words possible, the truth is that we have all left ash from fiery exchanges with the ones we love the most.

Words are *power-full,* and have the ability to swing either way, like a pendulum. They can uplift, motivate, inspire, and even heal when served up with the right intentions. The flip side is that they also have a branding power that can leave deep wounds and scars that feel as if they will never heal.

When you engage in word medicine, you are speaking mindfully and, most importantly, you are conscious of what you say and how it will affect others. What we say to our beloved sticks! All the good stuff—and all the hurtful things too. If you can claim words as a part of your healing medicine in the world, you can be aware that everything you say is in high vibration, bursts with positivity, and leaves others hanging on every word.

YOURSELF

Let us start with a question for you to ponder: what has your relationship to loving words been, throughout your life? Did your parents say how much they love you on a regular basis, how wonderful you are, and how grateful they are to have you in their lives? Or were they more rigid with their love blessings, only sharing their emotions with you sparingly? These truths will affect how easily you give affirmations to others and share or withhold your proclamations of love. This is a basic love 101 tip: *everyone* likes to hear how much they are loved. Even those who say they don't, really do. We all like to feel special, valued, and recognized for our special talents in the world.

More than just the love thoughts, however, lies the bigger truth that an inherent part of word medicine is how we communicate with our beloved, our children, and the greater world around us. Therefore, if you have yet to look at the way you communicate as medicine that you are doling out with every word, it's time to stop and evaluate, and take it up as if you are getting paid! This is because how we communicate is everything. It's the foundation of how we live in the world, and the core of our connection with each other.

If you are not very good at this, just PRACTICE! If you are quiet in your relationship and choose not to speak your fears or worries, start sharing. If you are angry and speak in loud, yelling tones, soften up and look for the gold in the situation, to help you calm down and speak with love and care. The point is that, wherever you are on the communication continuum, there is always room to be your better self tomorrow—so practice, and let your words be your currency of love.

THE COUPLE

Stand in your truth for a moment, and think back to things you have said to your beloved that you wish you had not. Everyone has demons, and it's better to look them in the eye than cower behind them in shame. Sometimes things just fly out of the mouth like fire, scorching everything in sight, and sometimes they are wielded with piercing precision to wound and even kill.

Knowing and acknowledging our shadow side is the key to healing and realizing our potential to be better and do better by our love. We all have things that still linger—for example, your beloved came home late, and instead of just having a conversation about that, you jump to, "… so you must be having an affair!" as if coming home late is an immediate pass to discussing your insecurities around fidelity.

This happens when deep wounds are not healed, and this is precisely when the dragon wants to get feisty. When you actively practice word medicine, however, you can chart a new course. You can *choose* just to say, "Hi, my love, you are late—is everything okay?" This is a simple statement and question, without emotional charge, based on love. This will set off the conversation in a whole new way, and you do not have to go down the negative-vibration road. Remember that your words have the power to heal and create beauty between you. If you get skilled at this art, the magic will unfold before your very eyes!

HEART WORK: *Use Your Words to Heal*

The way we speak can transform any situation into love or anger. You know that is true. In the heat of the moment, however, we may struggle to find the love in our hearts to speak to our beloved so that they feel heard and not attacked. Sometimes words have been broken, and we need to fix them and restore their original meanings, so that when you say "I love you" to your beloved it has actual depth and does not mean the same thing as, for example, "I love baseball." When you practice word medicine, you are speaking from love—the deepest meaning of love—and not ego, which often gets in the way of sharing love.

IDEAS AND PRACTICES

Understanding your beloved's needs

To truly love someone, you must seek to understand their needs, desires, and sufferings. You must strive to offer them words that will soothe them and transmit your compassionate care for their heart rather than sting or wound them. Sometimes we "don't mean to" say the one thing that upsets our beloved even more than they may already be upset, but the nonmeaning can still be hurtful. You must go back to the school of your beloved's heart to learn more about what they need in the moment rather than what you think they need. This is true love, and the highest calling of anyone's soul.

When your beloved is upset about anything, go to them and say, "I can see you are suffering, my love—how can I be of service to you? I want to help you in a way that feels good to you."

When you start to go down a road where you know it will end in a fight, take three deep breaths and say, "I can see my ego is invested in this conversation in a way that may be hurtful; I would like to take a moment and restore my compassionate heart in order to say what I need to say, with love." Then take a moment or two, until you are ready to do just that.

pairings

- Rumi's poetry: reading poetry can help you dive deeper into romance and words of love to use when you really want to come from love and not ego. And Rumi drips with romance, so—bonus!

- Throat-chakra essence: an essence is a vibrational medicine made from plants, crystals, and other energies, and you can take a dropper of this throat-chakra version (search online for "throat-chakra essence") when you are working with word medicine and needing to get clear and heal any past wounds around communication.

Journal on Word Medicine

Use this space to journal about your daily practices with word medicine. How are you growing through ego to speak from love?

_____

_____

_____

_____

_____

_____

_____

_____

_____

_____

_____

_____

_____

_____

_____

_____

_____

Naked Time

intimate physical connection

Anni and I wanted to remove
anything that stood between us,
physical or otherwise....

~TIM DAULTER,
describing the origins of "naked time"
as a relationship practice

Naked Time, a full-body embrace while completely naked, is a powerful practice that has served us well in times when we wanted to build connection in a very powerful way. Naked Time is not sex, and does not need to lead to sex, but uses skin-on-skin physical contact to strengthen the emotional and energetic bond between lovers.

YOURSELF

Skin-to-skin contact is well known to be an important part of human bonding, especially with babies and their parents. It results in lower levels of stress and higher levels of oxytocin, which creates those yummy feelings of happiness and well-being. A quick online search will give you a long list of studies about the necessity of human touch and skin-to-skin contact in children and adults.

However, in our relationship work, we see many couples in which one partner is resistant to the concept of Naked Time, usually because they have become completely turned off to sex with their beloved, and they equate nakedness with sex in their minds. As mentioned above, Naked Time is not sex; it is a different practice.

If you are the one who lacks a desire for sex with your beloved, then use Naked Time as a practice to begin to rekindle the physical connection that has been lost. If you desire physical intimacy and it is your partner who seems turned off to it, be compassionate and gentle in this practice. If sexual intercourse is difficult for your partner at this point, summon the inner strength to stick to this practice and enjoy the wonderful feelings of bonding without getting caught up in the heat of the moment and pushing for more.

The continued practice of Naked Time will reopen a connection between the two of you that will naturally flow into more felt intimacy in all aspects of your relationship—including the physical.

THE COUPLE

In virtually all of the relationships that we see, when the couple remembers back to the beginning, they describe a strong connection and bond. When two people have a strong bond, all types of interactions flow naturally, including hand-holding, staring deeply into each other's eyes, frequent sex, lots of cuddling, hugging and kissing, etc. As your connection fades over time, these interactions also fade, and you don't do them as often—or ever—anymore.

Energy works in all directions, however. So if you begin to implement as daily practices the things that came so naturally in the beginning of your relationship, your connection with your beloved will begin to strengthen and rebuild. Therefore, even if Naked Time feels a bit uncomfortable for you, or if any of the practices feels forced and less than genuine, that is typical and perfectly fine. Take up Naked Time as a gift to your beloved, as a gift to yourself, and as a gift to everyone in the world who looks up to you or sees you as a role model, because the positive effects on you and your relationship from building this connection benefit the lives of every person with whom you come into contact.

HEART WORK: *Prioritize Connecting with Your Beloved*

Once you have made the decision to supercharge the growth of your relationship and your connection with your beloved through Naked Time, the heart work is all in the follow-through. You need to start with a strong intention to be open, and to have a strong desire to live this practice. If you begin the work in internal resistance, it will be difficult to successfully implement the practice on a daily basis. This also relates to your priorities; if your life is busy, if you and your beloved are on different schedules, if you have children who cosleep with you, or any of a million other excuses, it might be easy to not follow through on this practice. However, with love and strong intention, anything can be worked out.

When Anni and I first took up this practice, we had three children who coslept with us, and we had very different schedules. However, we made it a priority by temporarily moving the kids out of our bed, taking planned breaks from our other work, and spending fifteen to twenty minutes in deep connection. We did this because it was necessary to create the type of relationship that we wanted for ourselves—and it paid off. Be very conscious about your priorities, and decide to put your relationship first, because what is more important to your quality of life than a strong love connection with your beloved?

IDEAS AND PRACTICES

Naked Time

Spend at least fifteen minutes each day in a deep, snuggling embrace with your beloved while you are both completely naked. Skin-to-skin contact is the only requirement; talking, fondling, giggling, laughing, or follow-up sex are all optional.

PAIRINGS

- Super-soft sheets and blankets. If you are going to lie naked together, do it in luxurious comfort! You can get what our family calls "softie blankets" to line your bed and cover you at a general-merchandise big-box store at a reasonable price. Make it a delicious, sensory experience from both the skin-to-skin snuggling and the softness that surrounds you.

- Song: "Amrit Naam" by Bachan Kaur. Instead of setting a timer to signal the end of your Naked Time session, use a song. This song from Kaur's Album *Soul Songs* is soothing, high-vibration music that will add to the atmosphere and effectiveness of your practice.

Journal on Naked Time

Use this space to journal about how
you feel during and after Naked Time,
and how this practice is affecting your
connection.

_____

_____

_____

_____

_____

_____

_____

_____

_____

_____

_____

_____

_____

_____

_____

Sex

a powerful ritual that can either
strengthen a bond or tear apart a relationship

You can reach rare peak states

of openness and connection

during lovemaking, but a

constant focus on lust and sex

can trap you in low vibration.

~TIM DAULTER

Passionate lovemaking is a natural extension of the deep connection forged by two people in love. When experienced as an expression of the pure emotion of love, care, and desire to give to your beloved, it allows the opportunity to escape your rational, intellectual mind, transcend the material world, and experience spiritual union with your beloved and with the Divine. This is the basis of the practice of tantra.

However, when sex is practiced as an individual, pleasure-seeking, and self-focused act, it can become a major negative issue in a relationship. We often see couples where one person has a stronger physical sex drive, and the other person sees their partner's drive for sex as selfishness and a symbol of the lack of care in their relationship. In other words, "I feel my beloved values his own orgasm over my feelings." When connection is lost in a relationship, one or both people will often have difficulty even thinking about physical intimacy, let alone practicing it.

YOURSELF

Being human brings the gift of having a dual nature—you are a spiritual being residing in a physical body. Your spiritual nature wants to rise to the heights of peace and joy, and seeks to unite with the Divine. In addition, your physical (animal) nature wants to meet its own basic needs of food, shelter, sex, security, and ego. Even though these two natures can seemingly be in conflict, they are a wonderful gift because the interplay between them helps you learn, grow, and strengthen, so that you can raise your vibration to transcend lower states of being. In addition, the places where you have open wounds and still need to heal become apparent on this path.

Without understanding and focusing on the fact that you are primarily a spiritual being on a journey of ascension, it is easy to get caught in the immediate lower-vibration urges of your physical body, with the sex drive being one of the strongest urges in many of us.

Take a real and honest look at how you feel about your sexual relationship with your beloved. If you are not interested in sex, look to the deeper reasons, and then take steps to heal them. If lack of connection is the problem, take up practices to build connection. If you need healing from previous relationships or prior abuse, then do the release work and take the steps toward healing what you need for your own wholeness.

If you desire more sex in your relationship, then look at how you present to your beloved. Do you engage in your sexual relationship from a place of love and giving and desiring pleasure for your partner, or are you primarily interested in your own orgasm? Come from a place of selfless giving and concern for them, to raise your own vibration and contribute to raising theirs. Love is about selfless giving, but the funny thing is that when you give unconditionally without an expectation of return, you end up receiving so much more in the end.

One very strong note of caution: if you experience a strong sexual drive and feel that it is not being met, then masturbation using pornography or fantasies of people other than your beloved is not a constructive way to deal with this. The more energy you feed into your sexual desires, the stronger they will become, and the energy that you put into fantasizing about people other than your beloved creates an energetic connection to the idea of the fantasy person and energetically destroys your relationship connection. All of these things will keep you mired in low vibration, damage your relationship, and take you further away from a Sacred Relationship in which you experience the intense pleasure (both physical and emotional) that far transcends mindless, physical sex.

THE COUPLE

A dynamic that we often see in relationships is a mismatch in sexual desire. Quite often both people enjoyed a passionate and frequent sexual relationship early in the relationship, but after the initial "honeymoon" period wears off, the lovemaking dwindles.

As challenges present in the relationship and connection suffers, we often see that one partner's desire for sex will decrease, while the other partner still feels the strong physical drive for orgasm and release. This mismatch in desire and perspective can lead to resentment on both sides, and further plunges the relationship into lack of connection and low vibration.

The good news is that with strong intention and a commitment to love, this dynamic can be avoided or repaired.

HEART WORK: *Giving Freely*

The work on the table, when it comes to improving your sexual connection, is to shift from focusing on your own desires to focusing on what would please your beloved. Determine what they want, and go the extra mile to give it to them. Whether it is romance and candles, a sensual massage with delicious oils, sexy lingerie, or fun role-playing, make the effort to give freely. When you are focused on your love for your partner and giving them what they desire, the high vibrations from your intentions will heal you both, and they are more likely to be motivated to give it back to you in kind—and maybe even more!

IDEAS AND PRACTICES

Sensual body massage

This can be a wonderful gift to a stressed-out partner. Give a long, loving massage with wonderful-smelling oils to decompress you both from the stresses of everyday life and anxieties. After covering all of the major muscle groups, you can work to more stimulating areas. Include at least thirty minutes of foreplay massage to transform your energies and get you both in the mood and the flow.

Do some research

There are tons of books, magazines, and articles with lots of how-to advice and ideas for stimulating and satisfying your lover. Variety is the spice of life. The main rule for great sex is to always, and in all ways, take your time. So whether it is lightly running your fingers over her entire body, or a new way to touch him that you haven't done before, the effort shows that you care, and can bring some new excitement to your sex life! Don't forget the possibility of bringing some toys out to play. A strong vibrator, soft feather, or another aid could be just what the doctor ordered.

Start your foreplay above the neck

Getting into the mood and out of the daily worries and stresses can start long before you reach the bedroom. Little poems, a dedicated song, suggestive text messages, or sultry voicemails can get the blood flowing and create some anticipation for the fun to come.

Sacred Kiss

The Sacred Kiss is an amazing connection exercise. Sit in a comfortable position with your beloved, put on a romantic song, and then have a make-out session for the length of the song. A kiss like this can be more intimate and meaningful than sex. As with many of the connecting exercises, allow your mind to stop and focus on what you are feeling—the texture of your beloved's lips on yours, the warmth in your heart, the heat rising in other places....

pairings

- "Good Love" massage oil by Everyone body oils. This amazing massage oil has just the right mixture of essential oils to make your room (and your beloved) smell amazing.
- Book: *Urban Tantra: Sacred Sex for the Twenty-First Century* by Barbara Carrellas. Check out this book for a hip and modern take on the spiritual science of tantra with a modern-day sensibility.

Journal on Sex

Use this space to journal about your feelings about your sex life. Take time to write down how you each like to be touched, and possible new ways to stimulate and spice everything up!

_____

_____

_____

_____

_____

_____

_____

_____

_____

_____

_____

_____

_____

_____

_____

_____

_____

_____

_____

SECTION THREE

WE

Envision

LOVE IS SPIRIT-QUESTING

To dream big fills the hearts of lovers with destiny, passion, and desire.

So goes the love warrior.

To take up the quest of love like a spirit master is the only way to the heart.

So goes the love warrior.

To envision a love beyond the heavens and strive to touch it is brave.

So goes the love warrior.

To bow at the feet of love, looking up into the eyes of your twin soul, is cosmically divine.

So goes the love warrior.

To give freely without expectation or keeping score is honorable.

So goes the love warrior.

To shine the light on love as the highest calling, and to move mountains to hold your beloved, is romantic.

So goes the love warrior.

To allow space for the other to grow and blossom is selfless.

So goes the love warrior.

Taking Stock

letting your beloved know how you really feel

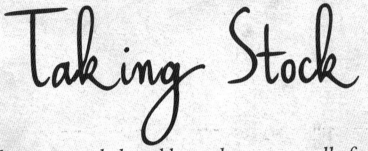

It is quite clear that between
love and understanding there
is a very close link....

~PAUL TOURNIER,
To Understand Each Other

Taking stock in your relationship means paying attention to how you really feel. Understanding your own wounds and injuries, how they affect your feeling toward your beloved, and what you want is a critical first step before you can truly envision your future and how to get there. Helping your beloved understand how you feel can open their heart to your reactions, and give them a chance to assist in your healing.

YOURSELF

So often we don't have a *real* think about our feelings and reactions; we stay at the level of "this feels bad" or "I don't like this," or we embrace vague feelings of resentment or detachment. The healing necessary to take our lives and relationships to the next level requires a understanding of what causes these feelings. Once you understand the source of your hurts and negativity, you can begin to take steps to release and heal yourself. Additionally, being able to share these personal insights with your beloved gives them an opportunity for heightened understanding and compassion, which can lead to changed behaviors.

THE COUPLE

There are always potential pitfalls when we attempt to communicate sensitive truths about what hurts us, and what we wish were different in our relationship. It is incredibly easy for any of us to become defensive when we hear our beloved saying what we do that hurts them. It is easy to go down the road of "they don't really love me" when we hear how we've triggered their struggles.

It is critically important that when you begin to share your insights about how you feel, your partner finds a way to listen to your feelings without taking your statements as personal attacks— and that you find a way to do the same. This takes us back to the beginning, where we suggest that Sacred Relationships are born with compassion and grow with empathy. Lean into trying to understand why your beloved may feel as they do, rather than judging or resisting their feelings.

HEART WORK: *Healing Requires Openness*

It is important for you both to realize that open communication about what you feel about your connection is a necessary step to improving your relationship. You can help to clear up misunderstandings and lay the groundwork for healing for both of you by being open and interested in what they are thinking and feeling. In addition, go deep within yourself to gain clear insight as to what holds you back, what shadow elements are alive in you, and what needs to be released so that nothing can interfere in your Sacred Relationship.

IDEAS AND PRACTICES

Our "Taking-Stock Questionnaire" (see below) lets you explore questions to stimulate your thoughts about your relationship. The "Crossing-the-Bridge Meditation Exercise" is good for developing compassion and seeing through your beloved's eyes.

TAKING-STOCK QUESTIONNAIRE

Take a journal to a quiet place and sit by yourself to complete or answer each of these prompts. Then get together with your beloved and discuss your answers. Reverse roles, and repeat the process. The questions are as follows:

- My biggest complaint about our relationship is:
- I feel that my beloved is most loving toward me when they:
- My beloved feels loved by me when I:
- I feel that my beloved is hurtful toward me when they:
- My beloved feels hurt by me when I:
- My beloved's most loving act of service toward me was:
- My beloved's most hurtful act that still lives in me was when:
- How much time per week do I spend thinking and focusing on my positive versus my negative feelings toward my beloved? Positive: _____ percent. Negative: _____ percent.

CROSSING-THE-BRIDGE EXERCISE

Sit in a quiet place where you won't be disturbed. Close your eyes and follow your breath in and out for a few minutes to come to a relaxed state. Then make the following journey:

- Picture yourself standing on the edge of a cliff. As you look out across the valley, you see your beloved standing on a cliff on the other side, facing away toward the horizon.

- You notice a small rope bridge connecting the sides. You step out and begin to walk across the bridge. You get to the other side and walk up behind your beloved.

- You put your arms around them and nuzzle against the side of their head. You look up and stare out at the same horizon that they are looking at. Now you see everything through their eyes. You see what it was like to grow up as they did, to have their childhood experiences—the traumas, the successes—everything. You see how these experiences have shaped them and still live with them today.

- Then you see their adult experiences through their eyes. You feel every feeling that they have felt—all that has happened, and how that has shaped them. You see everything that has occurred in your relationship through their eyes, feeling what they have felt. You understand why they have reacted as they have, and what still lives in them. You see and feel clearly everything that has happened to them, how that has made them feel, what still lives in them, and how that affects your relationship today.

- You give them a kiss and a squeeze, and then head back to the bridge and cross to your side again. You take one last look across at them, knowing that you have a better and deeper appreciation and understanding of them.

- When you are ready, open your eyes and write down any thoughts or feelings that you have about this experience.

pAirings

- Crystal: Eilat stone. This crystal is a strong aid to your throat chakra, the center of communication abilities including speaking, listening, and understanding. You can carry one with you to assist in healthy sharing between you.

Journal on Taking Stock

Use this space to journal about your feelings from the Taking-Stock Questionnaire—what you need to heal yourself, and what you can give to your beloved to help their healing.

_____

_____

_____

_____

_____

_____

_____

_____

_____

_____

_____

_____

_____

_____

_____

_____

_____

_____

_____

Spiritual Divorce

a fresh start

No matter how difficult the past,
you can always begin again today.

~JACK KORNFIELD

We will now dive into the dark and difficult places within your relationship closet that truly need to be cleaned out, refreshed, and blessed with love and forgiveness. The purpose of a Spiritual Divorce is clear out the old energies that hold your relationship where it is now, so that you are free to consciously create the relationship that you want.

The ability to let go of attachment to the old ways and the relationship in its current state is within your ability, and is absolutely necessary to take your relationship to the next level of happiness. Letting go is not a loss, but can create an opening, a space for newness to grow and blossom. Do not be fearful of releasing attachments to whatever does not serve your relationship.

YOURSELF

The first step to clearing out the negativity that lives in your relationship is to decide that you will let go of everything that holds it in a low-vibration state. The symbolic action that we take to make this intention manifest is what we call a "Spiritual Divorce." The road to envisioning something new starts with letting go of the old.

This is a symbolic act, not a real divorce, so please allow yourself to release any fear of the word "divorce" and understand that this practice is simply a refreshing cleansing of your relationship. As you try this on, like an itchy sweater, it may not feel comfortable at first; but trust that it will serve a higher purpose in the end. Use this tool for what it is intended for—a true first start.

Notice how you feel after you participate in the Spiritual Divorce. Are you sad, relieved, open? What stirred within you as you moved through this experience? Just notice, without judgment. Make sure that you take time away from your partner to be with trusted friends or by yourself, to do some deep reflecting after your Spiritual Divorce. This time away from each other is necessary to create the space needed to recommit to each other with a new, shared vision.

THE COUPLE

Every couple has struggles; it is how you handle struggle that determines the strength and happiness of your relationship. Over time, little quirks can turn into a breakdown of communication, which can build up years of resentment and spoken and unspoken hurts. So many couples say to each other, "Let's just start over," and while that may work for a few days, soon the old habits and thought patterns return.

If you have a large, infected wound, you can say that you won't let it bother you, but as long as it remains unhealed the pain will affect you, and likely worsen. Similarly, without intentional cutting of the connection to and healing of old hurts, discontent slowly creeps back into the relationship like a heavy fog, and soon the couple is blinded by old hurts again without a clear path to escaping them.

Spiritual Divorce is an intentional way to bring form and ceremony to the ending of an old paradigm, in order to release and heal old wounds and reshape the relationship to reflect new vows and sacred practices.

HEART WORK: *Letting Go of the Past*

A spiritual divorce is meant to help your heart connection grow once you have had an opportunity to wipe the energetic slate clean. This is not easy work, and it can feel very real. This can feel like you are jumping off an emotional cliff—and in some ways it is. It involves incredible trust, and a desire to really elevate the relationship to a new level. In matters of the heart, it is always best to operate from trust and deep listening to one's inner knowing.

Create a Spiritual Divorce

We will do this in four steps:

1. Cleansing of the rings

2. Cutting the cord

3. Intention meditation

4. New vows

1. Cleansing of the Rings. Prepare a small bowl of rosewater, and place it on your Relationship Altar. If you have other items, such as crystals, to promote energetic clearing, place them around or in the bowl. You and your beloved will both remove your wedding or commitment rings (engagement rings, anniversary bands, etc.) and place them in the rosewater. If you are not married, or do not have rings, you can use some other symbols of your relationship. (If water would damage these items, you can use sage instead of water for cleansing.)

Together, hold the strong intention that, by removing these rings and symbolically cleansing them with the water, they are being cleared of any negative and/or low-vibration energy that has developed throughout your relationship. Leave the rings in the rosewater overnight.

The next day, remove the rings from the water and dry them, but leave them on the altar. Do not put them on again until after you have made new vows to each other. When you dry your rings, clean and polish them with the intention of scrubbing away all low-vibration energies. You can use baking soda or toothpaste (the white kind, not a gel) and a paper towel to bring back a nice shine to them. Lastly, you can use white sage to cleanse the rings. Light the sage, and pass the rings through the smoke to energetically cleanse them.

2. Cutting the Cord. The next step in your spiritual divorce is a cutting-the-cord ceremony. For this you will need a piece of red cord or yarn about three feet long, and two pairs of scissors. Each of you will tie one end of the cord to the other's left wrist, so that you are joined by the cord. Try not to tie it too tightly or too loosely, as you will be wearing this cord as bracelets until you are both ready to make new vows to one another.

Once you are tied together, left hand to left hand, each of you picks up a pair of scissors, looks into the other's eyes, and says, one at a time, "By cutting this cord I dissolve our relationship as it is, so that I may create a Sacred Relationship with you in conscious awareness and love." Then, by signaling with a nod of the head, both of you cut the cord with your scissors at the same time. Once the cord is cut, look into each other's eyes and say, "We are now spiritually divorced." Trim the ends of the cord close to the knot so that you now have a bracelet, a reminder of your Spiritual Divorce that you will wear until you create a new commitment to one another.

3. Intention Meditation. Now that you are spiritually divorced, take the time you both need to try on this new relationship state, and notice how it feels. Without judgment, notice how it feels to have energetic space between you. Take some physical time to be away from one another to journal, touch in with nature, meditate, and envision what you want your new Sacred Relationship to look like.

As you continue to journey through this book, you will be guided through specific ways to do release and healing work. As you vision your new relationship, write out new vows for it and decide how long you need before you want to approach your partner with your intentions for your future together. Both of you should be engaged in this process, and decide mutually how long you both need before you are ready to recommit to one another.

4. New Vows. After you have taken the time you need to meditate on how you feel, and have started to envision your new journey with your beloved, choose a time when you can exchange new vows. You can make this a special ceremony where you get dressed up or go away with each other for a night, so that you have some exclusive time together.

Choose special paper on which to write out your new vows, so that you can read them without forgetting all the important details of what you wanted to say, and then gift the paper to your beloved. Cut the Spiritual-Divorce bracelets off of each other's wrists, and then read your new vows to each other. This signifies the fresh new start you are about to embark upon.

pairings

- Rose quartz crystal: rose quartz crystals represent love, and hold the vibration of open-heart space. You can either wear rose quartz around your neck or carry one in your pocket while you are going through the Spiritual Divorce. This will help keep your heart open to love and trust as you make this transition.
- Song: "Love is Messy" by Nina Lee.

Journal on Spiritual Divorce

Use this space to draft your new vows, and reflect on how it felt to do the Spiritual Divorce.

_____

_____

_____

_____

_____

_____

_____

_____

_____

_____

_____

_____

_____

_____

_____

_____

_____

Brotherhood

real conversation with men

A mystic bond of brotherhood

makes all men one.

~THOMAS CARLYLE

At our Sacred Relationship live retreats, we spend most of an entire day with all of the men together, separate from the women. We have found this to be one of the most powerful and transformative experiences for the men. In our society, men gather to watch or play sports, drink beer, and other "social" traditions. However, where in our culture is it practiced, or even acceptable, for men to gather and have real conversations about the important things going on in their lives? Forging a brotherhood that serves as a solid foundation for men to share and seek consel from one another is a transformative healing tool—and a safe place to connect, laugh, and bond.

YOURSELF

It has been said that "no man is an island," but we all too often try to live without the support of other men. If we are having difficulty in our relationships, if we feel confused about life direction, or if we just feel lost, whom can we talk to? The fact that our culture has no tradition of men sitting together in a circle of brotherhood, sharing and listening to each other, being accountable and supporting each other, undermines the foundation of our being.

Creating this outlet in a man's life is a critical step in your personal growth. However, this will require you to be strong enough to step out of our society's prohibition against men having feelings and expressing them to other men.

We all have areas where we struggle—and that is okay. We all have been hurt, and have hurt other people. We all have minds and hearts that think and feel. Unless we find our circle of brothers to open up to, we won't be able to reach our full potential as human beings, and all of the pent-up emotions and worries will express themselves in low-vibration ways.

THE COUPLE

Incorporating brotherhood into your life as a support system will allow a necessary outbreath in your relationship, reducing the pressure to be each other's sole support system. You will have others to help give you perspective, and keep you walking your talk and rooted in your resolve.

When we hold brotherhood circles at the live Sacred Relationship retreats, we commonly get feedback about how nice it is to hear the commonalities in the issues shared among all of the men—just the simple knowledge that many others deal with similar challenges. This feedback reveals how desperate we are for such council, and how being able to openly share our issues and concerns is a huge relief. Having your voice be heard, sharing and gaining insight about your past wounds, being witnessed, and sending energy out to the Great Mystery in a brotherhood circle radiates healing into the world, and has a deepening effect on your relationship.

HEART WORK: *Creating Brotherhood*

Tim runs Sacred Brotherhood retreats, and at one of these one of the attendees was going through a very difficult time in his life, including struggling in his relationship. The call went out to other men who attended that workshop, and this man who had never had a support network in his entire life was immediately in contact with eight of his brothers on a daily basis by phone, text, and email. One of them had even gone through the same situation and could speak directly to his experiences. The brotherhood provided our friend a fresh perspective, unwavering support, and heartfelt love that truly contributed to his healing and recovery from this life trauma.

IDEAS AND PRACTICES

Attend a sweat lodge

A sweat lodge is a Native American purification ceremony that provides a sacred space to release, pray, and dream-travel. Many indigenous or native teachers offer men-only sweats. These are great places to meet like-minded men in an environment where you can make connections, speak honestly, and dive deeper into your spiritual destiny.

Join or start a local men's circle

The call of the brotherhood has been shot into the universe by the bow of transformative healing, and as a result, men's circles are forming and change is happening. Try attending one of our Sacred Brotherhood retreats to experience the magic of men's circles and councils. Afterwards, you will be armed and ready to bring this sacred medicine back into your community.

Fire circles are also a gateway to sacred councils, and a container for transformative work such as release, to help your community re-root and answer the call of the ancestors. There may already be established men's groups, regular fire circles, or sweat lodges in your local area. Use what is accessible to you to connect with other men in sacred council, and take up transformative work to help your community re-root and answer the call of the ancestors.

pAIRINGS

- Palo santo wood: palo santo produces a fragrant smoke when burned, which can be used to clear your energy at the beginning of a men's circle, or any time you need a quick cleanse and a high-vibe jolt!

- *Native Spirit Oracle Cards* by Denise Linn. This is a card deck that we use at all of the Sacred Brotherhood Retreats to help us hear Spirit speaking to us. The cards that you pull are not random; they always show up for a reason—look for how these cards and their meanings speak to you. You can either pull one card in the morning for the day or use one of the multicard reading formats in the beginning of the guidebook that comes with the cards.

Journal on Brotherhood

Define "brotherhood" for yourself. Use this space to journal about where and how you can find a tribe that will hold space for you.

_____

_____

_____

_____

_____

_____

_____

_____

_____

_____

_____

_____

_____

_____

_____

_____

_____

_____

Sisterhood

lean into the tribe

There's one thing stronger
than magic: sisterhood.

~ROBIN BENWAY

Sisterhood is a legacy that acts as a balm for suffering, and thrives in hope and prosperity. Women are waking to find an intense yearning for companionship and support on this uphill road toward equality and social justice. Sisterhood is defined as a group of women linked by common interests, shared concerns, and real blood bonds, and there are soul needs that are filled by communion with a circle of women. These women are the ones who will hold you up, laugh and cry with you, witness you, allow you space to dream and be heard, and truly honor the woman you are.

A sisterhood is a much-needed wellspring of inspiration, so if you do not belong to a tribe of sacred sisters, seek one out in your area. Women's Moon Circles are popping up everywhere, and that is a great place to start your search. Having a circle beyond your relationship with your beloved is a gift to both of you, and gives you space to stretch and grow. Being free enough to take the time and space you need to fill your cup allows you to come back to the relationship with fresh eyes, a vibrant heart, and new perspectives.

YOURSELF

As part of self-care, being in a sisterhood circle can help provide balance and clarity to your life, and get you charged up to take on any challenges that come your way. It fills your fun tank, lights your fire, and helps you live in expansive community rather than isolation. As you work on your relationship with your beloved, you can bring to it many of the intentional skills that you glean from sitting in council with women, and these gifts could greatly improve the energy exchange between you.

Week 19 was about Brotherhood, as it is equally important for men to come together and be heard and seen by each other. At the Sacred Relationship live retreats, we have a day where the men and women are separated and each group does sacred work without the other. This is typically one of the favorite days for the couples, because they are allowed space to be with their own tribe and see that they are not alone on their quest to better their relationships. They uncover shared struggles, which are heard with common ears and responded to with empathy.

Take some time to reflect on your experiences with girls and women when you were growing up. Were you fortunate enough to be in sacred circles—sharing, learning ancient wisdoms from your elders, and being honored for transitions in your life? Or were you in regular competition with them, trying to one-up the other in order to fit into the societal paradigm that we must be mean to each other? This is an outdated way of thinking, and there is no place for that ideology in your life. Sisterhood is healing—so find a tribe, and be grateful that you did.

THE COUPLE

The antidote to routine, boredom, and repetition is a fresh perspective. Giving your relationship room for expansive exhalation creates nourished room for the inhalation when you come back together. You do not exist entirely in the orbit of your beloved; rather, you are two separate beings coming together to create a relationship that fulfills a soul contract and brings magic to the world that only the two of you can ignite.

In order to allow that destiny to unfold, you need to let the winds of inspiration dance between you, opening up space to make room for cocreation. Spending time in sisterhood is one way to foster that alchemical design. In ancient days, women and men would council separately from each other to share stories of rites of passage, task each other with accountability for showing up in the world armed with their personal brand of medicine, and witness each other's triumphs and pains.

These separate councils were sacred because each sex had private dreams whispered to them by the Great Mystery that were for their ears only. This was not only acceptable but expected. We need to bring back sitting together in circles in sisterhood and brotherhood; the ancients knew what they were doing, and we need to do this once again, and listen to the whispers.

HEART WORK: *Gathering Heals*

Separating from your beloved may seem counterintuitive, but this small kind of release is a gift that makes room for the whole you to show up and shine. Commit to this self-care task, and take some time away from your relationship on a regular basis. Spend time with your circle, share stories with your sisters, learn how you are connected as women by blood and to the moon, and listen and be listened to.

Building a Sacred Relationship is not for the faint-hearted; it requires heart work that will push you to your emotional limits. So you need a safe space to plug in your battery for recharging. And frankly, we need more places in the world where we can be seen and praised for the gifts we possess. Find the space you need to do the work that calls from your heart.

IDEAS AND PRACTICES

Pamper-Yourself Night, with homemade goodies!

Invite your tribe of sisters for a special night to create products to pamper yourselves! Here is one recipe to kick off a lovely night of self-care (see below).

CACAO AND HONEY MASK

- ⅓ cup raw cacao powder
- ⅓ cup plain yogurt
- ¼ cup finely ground oatmeal
- 3 tablespoons raw honey

Mix everything together until a smooth paste is formed. Apply to face and neck, leaving space around eyes. Leave on for fifteen minutes.

Rinse with warm water, and then finish with a gentle face oil.

Do a sisterhood fear release

Ask each woman to write down a fear that gets in the way of living her highest potential in this lifetime. Then burn the papers, one by one, each of you throwing them into a collective fire or a large or moving body of water. This is a very power-full ceremony when done in sisterhood, as it allows the women a place to bear witness to common pains, and pushes you personally forward to dance in your own shadow, be raw, and cleanse away your fears.

Make a necklace for your beloved

Invite your sisterhood to come over and create sacred necklaces for their beloveds while sharing your love stories around the circle with each other. This gives you all an opportunity to hear about the beauty that ignited each connection, which deepens the bonds between you and—bonus!—gives you a gift to share with your beloved afterward.

Witness dancing

Each woman chooses a song that inspires her, stands up in front of her tribe, and dances her heart out, witnessed by all other women present. This may sound scary at first, but in reality there is deep freedom in this ceremony, and it's a truly beautiful thing to watch women find their power through movement.

pairings

- Music: India.Arie, Mary Isis, and Nina Lee are all women artists who sing woman-identified music perfect for witness dancing and ceremony.
- Raw cacao from Navitas Naturals, a family-owned green business that produces an excellent raw, organic cacao powder.
- Oracle card deck: *Soulful Woman Guidance Cards: Nurturance, Empowerment and Inspiration for the Feminine Soul Cards* by Shushann Movsessian and Gemma Summers. This deck has gorgeous women-inspired

images, and speaks to the heart of sisterhood with each pull. Use this deck to pull a card every day to help you stay in conscious awareness and remind you of your connection to the greater sisterhood collective.

· I AM Sisterhood live retreat: consider joining Anni Daulter for a live I AM Sisterhood retreat. These retreats, held in various locations around the world, bring you together in sisterhood for life-changing experiences and help you tap into your soul's purpose in the world.

Journal on Sisterhood

Use this space to reflect on your connection to Sisterhood and how it serves you, and start unfolding some creative ideas for gathering with your sisterhood tribe.

_____

_____

_____

_____

_____

_____

_____

_____

_____

_____

_____

_____

_____

_____

_____

_____

_____

_____

_____

Ceremonial Mind

elevate the mundane

Many people are alive, but don't
touch the miracle of being alive.

~THICH NHAT HANH

Life passes in a myriad of flowing moments with the potential to wash through you unnoticed and unmarked. Another day spent walking next to your beloved, taking out the trash, cleaning dishes, driving to work, and eating lunch could be simply any old day. It is up to you to approach each moment with devotion to your task. It is your challenge to fill even the most mundane of tasks with clear, thoughtful awareness.

Like living in Divine Mind, the process of creating reverence in daily life involves the art of ceremony, and transforming simple mundane experiences into deeper knowing. Deepening your intentions, Ceremonial Mind asks you to soul-stretch even further, to start marking your life experiences with ritual and ceremony, so that you can truly live in a sacred reality.

YOURSELF

Entering Ceremonial Mind is a personal choice that requires accompaniment with action. Letting the tasks of daily life swirl around you without real connection or involvement strips them of their beauty and devalues their importance. When you consciously choose to enter Ceremonial Mind, you delve into your inner personal mysteries and deep, intuitive knowing, allowing your creative action to come to life. You are bearing witness to yourself, so that spontaneous right action can bubble up from your heart and body—like knowing the exact best moment for a hug, or taking time to mark special passing moments with ceremony.

It is time now to reflect on how you approach your daily living, and check in with yourself about how you celebrate sacred moments in your life. Do you let them pass you by, or do you find creative ways to mark them with reverence, care, and beauty—what we call "living in the Beauty Way"? Do you wake up next to your beloved as if it is the most precious thing happening in your life? Do you feed yourself with love and nourishment? Do you clean the dishes that held your breakfast as if they are treasures? Do you drive to work 100 percent in your body, noticing the wonders of the world all around you?

When you recognize that the smallest moments can expand your heart, you realize that there is no moment that is not sacred, and no moment that cannot be honored in ceremony. This is living in Ceremonial Mind.

THE COUPLE

In the mundane life, you may not always be able to see your beloved with joyful, loving eyes. You may choose to be angry or resentful about taking out the trash for the 500th time, or having THAT argument again, whatever "that" is for you. But if you choose to live in Ceremonial Mind, you create a fresh opportunity for viewing these moments in right relationship to the bigger plan that is directly connected to your soul contract with your beloved.

Ceremony does not only mean grand, elaborate rituals to celebrate big events in your life, but a way to simply honor small transitions, new traditions, endings, beginnings, successes, passings, and healings. Ceremonial Mind is married to the Beauty Way insofar as its foundation lies in intention, and it can only happen when you create space for such rituals with reverence, care, and beauty.

Decide to be alive and absorbed in presence with your beloved, so that more of these moments can surface in your connection. This commitment to the present makes time timeless, all possibilities possible, and real miracles happen. To begin to grow your Sacred Relationship with intentional love, start by making the conscious choice to live in mindfulness with each other, open yourself up to more sacred acts of service for one another, and take the time to mark various events with sweet ceremonies, small rituals, and loads of beauty.

HEART WORK: *Personal Retreat*

You are the celebrant of your life, and sometimes that means taking a personal retreat for yourself to tap into your creative action or your spirit guides, or even just to get clear on your relationship.

Each treasured moment of your life has meaning, whether you can see it in that moment or not. Allowing yourself time and space in personal retreat away from your beloved is a huge gift to the connection, as it allows you to get centered and refreshed, and to look deeply at how you serve your relationship to yourself and your beloved.

The concept of *mudita,* Sanskrit for "joy," suggests that when you live in full presence, you can find joy in all things and be in gratitude for them. Be joyful that you have hands so that you may touch your beloved, or eyes to see the beauty all around you. This joy is your right, and belongs to everyone. You and your beloved must share joy with each other, as that is one foundation of true love.

In a personal retreat, you can spend time meditating on how you share joy, and how that impacts your relationship.

IDEAS AND PRACTICES

Sacred Path Card *reading*

Jamie Sams has a Native American-inspired deck entitled *Sacred Path Cards,* which suits a soul-path card reading well. In the beginning of the book, she walks you through a reading to help you get on your right path. When you go on personal retreat, take time to do a sacred-path reading, and journal all of your thoughts and reflections.

Do it with joy

Take up all tasks with joy, and even say it out loud! "I am cooking with joy," "I am smiling with joy," "I am drawing a bath with joy," or "I am meditating with joy." Using this a daily mantra will infuse your present moment with the Sacred, and offer a teaching to those around you about living in Ceremonial Mind.

New traditions

Living in Ceremonial Mind gives you room to bring ceremony and new traditions to the table for any reason you want. You can start a tradition to have Saturday Sacred Nights, for example, where you have dinner with your family, light a special candle, and say a meditation or prayer over the meal. After dinner, you and your beloved can carve out time to spend together, envisioning and planning shared dreams. If you do this little sacred ceremony once a week, think about how much ritual and beauty will grace your home, and how much magic this will start to infuse into your life!

pairings

- Smile Meditation. This is a mindfulness practice to help raise your vibration and bring joyful intention to each moment. When you are out and about in your town, practice smiling at people— literally! SMILE AT EVERYONE who walks by you. This may feel forced in the beginning, but it brings you internal joy, and the more you practice, the less forced it will become. Smile at yourself as well!

- Book: *The Miracle of Mindfulness: An Introduction to the Practice of Meditation* by Thich Nhat Hanh. A wonderful book to take the concept of ceremonial mind deeper.

- *The Wild Unknown Divination Card Deck* by Kim Krans. This highly popular, beautiful tarot deck is easy to use and amazing to look at. It is great for beginners in tarot as well as to the highly trained reader.

Journal on Ceremonial Mind

Use this space to reflect about getting creative with ceremony! What events in your life do you want to start marking with ritual and ceremony? How can you elevate the mundane into Beauty-Way moments?

_____

_____

_____

_____

_____

_____

_____

_____

_____

_____

_____

_____

_____

_____

Release It

letting go of the past

Suffering is not holding you.
You are holding suffering. When
you become good at the art of
letting sufferings go, then you'll
come to realize how unnecessary it
was for you to drag those burdens
around with you.

~OSHO

We all have had transgressions and negative things happen to us in the past that may still be affecting us today. Maybe it was something that happened in our childhood, such as abuse or abandonment. Maybe it is what we were taught, or how we were treated, so that we still carry a belief that we are not good enough and will never amount to anything. Whether it was betrayal, abandonment, trauma, or some other emotional wound, we need to release it so that it does not control or limit who we are today or what we can be in the future.

YOURSELF

There is an Arab proverb that one should write anything bad that happens to them in the sand so that it can be easily erased. However, most of us carry wounds that are much harder to release. Anytime something happens to us that wounds our auric and spiritual bodies, especially if our emotional wounds or traumas are not resolved and processed, then the event lives in us as an energy pattern.

These bundles of low vibration live in our energetic body and cause harm to us in a variety of ways. They can block flows of energy, preventing us from manifesting the lives that we want or even causing physical disease. These old hurts can also be reactivated by sensitive interactions with others, and we may feel the pain again in such a real way that it is almost as traumatic as the original event.

If this happens to you, it can easily interfere with your current relationship; it can cause you to build up protective walls in an effort to avoid the pain. But in reality, this will only cut you off from new opportunities. The older and deeper the wound, the more energy it will take to release it. However, our reality is ultimately controlled by our minds, so it is within our power to let go and heal anything from our past—even trauma from previous lives.

THE COUPLE

At one of our early Sacred Relationship Retreats, we had a couple we will call Kathy and Ted, who had been married for about five years. They had gotten married in Las Vegas, and a few days after the wedding they were having angry words about something. Ted, in a thoughtless moment, said, "We should just turn around and go back to Vegas and get a divorce."

This careless statement lived so deeply in Kathy that she never got over it; it lived between them for five years. In fact, it was still so alive in Kathy that any time she talked about the incident she would burst into tears. Clearly, Kathy and Ted were not going to be able to put their relationship back together until this old wound was cleared and healed.

This is just one example; every couple that we have ever worked with has had old wounds that need unpacking and clearing out, either from before the relationship started or within the relationship (or both), that contributed to a negative dynamic between them.

HEART WORK: *Letting It Go*

Release begins with identifying whatever lives within you that does not serve your highest good, that holds you back, and that you want to let go of. Sometimes these things are obvious to you such as anger, impatience, hurt from the betrayal of an affair, etc. But many times the wounds that need to be released and healed are deeper, older, and invisible at first glance. Examples that we have seen include: allowing parents to control how you feel, developing low self-esteem, and experiencing traumas that you may not even remember.

Regardless of the type of energy to be released, the first and most important step is to absolutely decide to release it. If you still feel that you are entitled to your righteous anger at your partner after an affair, for instance, or if you find comfort in defining yourself as a victim of your parent's abuse or alcoholism, then you are not quite ready to release those negative energies from your life. To prepare for this work, you must pass through the following stages:

1. Identify what you will release;

2. Decide that you want to release those energies; and

3. Know that you will release them.

Once you have progressed to an unshakable knowing, in the bones of your being, that you will release that which does not serve you, you have already won. A final word of advice is that fear-releases, like onions, have layers. You will probably not do just one release and then be done with the issue for the rest of your life. For extremely deep and old wounds, it may take several release ceremonies to get rid of all the murky junk living within your spiritual body—but you *can and will* get there.

As you progress down this healing path, you may also turn over a few rocks and find more hidden wounds now ripe for release. Repeat these same steps to continue on your healing journey.

IDEAS AND PRACTICES

Guided writing

We described this exercise in Week 7 (on Trust). You can use the same process to ask your spirit guides for insight into what you need to release from your own personal life and from your relationship with your beloved. Each of you can individually seek counsel from your spirit guides to accomplish this task, and then come together to collectively shed past pains.

THROW IT AWAY

Release work is *energy work,* and utilizing nature for this ceremony is a very effective technique for releasing low-vibration shadows.

- Once you have identified what you want to dump from your spirit body, go into a place of nature such as the woods or a beach, and find a rock that calls to you. It should be big enough that you can write all the things that you want to release on it, but small enough that you can easily pick it up and cast it away to be transformed by Mother Earth. (Usually our retreat participants wish they had a bigger rock!)

- Write everything that you want to release onto the rock. Then gather all of the hurt, pain, and negativity within you, and energetically push it into the stone. Allow your emotional tenor to rise to a very high and excited state as you prepare to cast your pains into the unknown, away from you, for good! Then throw the rock full of these demons as hard and as far as you can, letting out a primal scream as you do it. This will force the negativity out of your body and back into the Earth, where it can be transformed and contained.

Once you have released these negative energies, you need to take a moment to ground yourself and fill up again with the high-vibration energy of pure love:

- Stand straight, and visualize the bright sun of the eighth chakra (about eighteen inches above your head).

- Sweep your arms out to your sides in a wide upward arc. When your arms meet above your head, grab the energy of your eighth chakra and pull it down into the top of your head.

- Feel it traveling down your spine, feeding every cell of your body with pure love. This will prevent any of the negativity that you just released from returning.

pairings

- Crystal: amethyst. Amethyst carries energies that support emotional release and healing. Wear it in a necklace or carry it on your person during release work, and for seven days after the release. You can also keep a piece of amethyst under your pillow at night to invite healing to occur during your dreamtime.

- Incense: sandalwood, honeysuckle, or juniper incenses are all excellent for supporting emotional healing. After your release, light the incense and sit in silent meditation to allow the healing work you have just done to process and complete itself.

Journal on Release It

Use this space to reflect on the release work that you have just done. How did you feel afterward, and what opportunities do you envision opening up for you as a result of this healing work?

_____

_____

_____

_____

_____

_____

_____

_____

_____

_____

_____

_____

_____

Romance Me

keep it fresh and sweet

Never underestimate the power
of a single rose shared.

~ANNI DAULTER

Surprises keep a relationship fresh, and romance keeps it sweet. Slow dances in the kitchen for no particular reason, impromptu massages, handpicked flowers left on the pillow with a love note, sweet texts sent to your beloved throughout the day—these are the small moments that have a big impact.

Romance happens naturally in the beginning of a love story, and at some point needs to shift to heart work. Time brings a natural fade of intensity to love stories, but the heart wants what the heart wants.

Couples get into trouble because they start remembering the phase of their relationship when little surprises happened with frequency and declarations of love were as easy as breathing—and they want that back. Rather than transitioning to practices and heart work, they tend to give up on each other, or look outside the relationship to fulfill that love-junkie fix that typically occurs only in the early days.

Dripping poetic-prose masters like Rumi and Shakespeare got it, and saw the value in the romantic word and accompanying action. You may not be a poetry guru, but you can refresh your love with little moments of sprinkled magic, and see how far and wide that takes you in the heart of your beloved.

YOURSELF

Romance is a particular vibration of love. It is love expressed through beauty and creativity, and typically offered up with an artistic hand. If one or both members of a couple are more practically oriented, or life becomes so demanding that you need every ounce of energy just to make the trains run on time, then whimsical and beautiful offerings for love and beauty's sake alone tend to take a back seat to the utilitarian. This is why romance is often lacking or completely missing from relationships.

We take the strong stance, however, that romance is vitally important to elevating your relationship to Sacred. Romance brings balance, color, and juicy vitality to you and the relationship. Be truthful—how smooth is your romantic game? If you struggle with this aspect of connection, it's okay, and it's not hopeless! There are loads of simple ways to keep romance fresh and alive; it just has to be awake in your consciousness and you have to be willing in your heart. Like any other skill or aspect of yourself that you are trying to expand, it takes practice, and at first it may feel awkward.

The most important aspects when you are bringing a romantic experience to your beloved are: 1) creativity and newness—don't bring flowers for the hundredth time and think that this alone is romance; and 2) effort—go out of your way to make your beloved see that they are valuable and important to you, and that you have thought about who they are and what they like. Remember, the gift of romance doesn't just feed them, it also helps you to open and grow in ways that will make you a happier, more creative, balanced person.

THE COUPLE

The death of the romantic due to the purely practical can cause huge rifts in your relationship if you or your beloved is a creative soul who highly honors beauty and romance in life. This can cause the relationship to suffer and wither away over years of neglecting this important aspect of love. It is also easy to interpret this starving of affection, effort, and creativity as a sign that your beloved does not value or care about what feeds you and your connection. This interpretation, however, piles more negative thinking and low vibration onto an already strained relationship.

Take up the practice of *right understanding,* and talk about your feelings with each other. If you understand the true dynamic, you may find that your beloved would like to give you what you want, but just doesn't have the tools to express it because they spent all day—and possibly most of their life—balancing spreadsheets, hanging drywall, or writing code. In taking up a Sacred Relationship, they will want to meet your needs and gift you with all the delicious aspects of love, and you will want to return this to them.

HEART WORK: *Make It Special*

Taking up the work of nurturing blossoming romance in your relationship is fun and rewarding if you do it right! Expanding your horizons to discover new romantic ideas, expressing yourself in fun and vibrant ways, and putting yourself out there can be stressful if you turn your back on these as opportunities for your own personal growth.

Don't take yourself too seriously, or stay tied to perfection or "rightness," as romance lives and breathes the air of surprise and drippy gestures that fill the love cup with goodness. Romantic gestures are meant to be decadent risks, so accept that upfront, and just dive into trying everything that you can think of to keep the spark alive. These moments will have a big impact on keeping smiles aplenty and flutters in the heart.

Take a leap—wear that sexy underwear, write a poem, cook a French meal, or leave chocolate and a love note on the pillow in the morning before you leave for work. Whatever it is, have fun, laugh, giggle, and do it all with a sense of adventure and abandon. Drench your offerings with beauty, caring, thoughtfulness, and generosity, as these are all forms of high-vibration energy exchanges and will naturally elevate your relationship.

From the receiving end, while thoughtful and gentle feedback can be helpful in guiding future efforts, be sparing with your critiques but wildly spend your gratitude, praise, admiration, and recognition of all efforts made. The Law of Attraction is always in effect, so vibrate at the frequency of what you want, and praise and gratitude will multiply abundance in your life.

When reinfusing romance into your relationship, you can start anywhere! It is easy to fall into the trap of wanting to pull off something so big that you never actually get to it. Start with small and doable ideas, and then move into the bigger gestures as you gradually build your romantic game back up. Make romance a highlight of your daily practices in even the smallest of ways, and you will see a huge impact on the overall quality of your relationship.

IDEAS AND PRACTICES

Create an evening just for your beloved

Plan an entire evening that is completely focused on what your beloved enjoys. Whether it is dinner at a fancy restaurant dressed to the nines, or an evening at home making crafts or making love, plan it out, get the babysitter, take a shower, get dressed nicely, smell great, and bring your A-game. You used to do it when you first met, so get back into that energy and enjoy every moment.

The little things matter

Do not underestimate the little gestures that will pack a big punch. If you take up romance as a daily practice, you will need your efforts to be sweet, swift, and surprising. Here are a few ideas to get your creative juices flowing:

- Have tea or coffee waiting by the bedside every morning with a little note or flower.
- Offer a foot rub after a long day at work.
- Draw a bath and fill it with flower petals; have beautiful music playing in the background, and candles lit for ambiance.
- Leave a little clue to a surprise hidden somewhere in your house for them to find after you have left for work.
- Send sexy sweet texts throughout the day when you are not together.
- Send love songs to your beloved, and say the words remind you of them.
- Say how attractive they look, and notice when they are wearing something new.
- Surprise them with a lunch date and maybe shopping for something new to wear out for your date that weekend.
- Plan date nights and walks on the beach or picnics in the park.
- Grab them and tell them how sexy they are; plant a delicious kiss on their neck when they least expect it.

pairings

- Book: *How to Romance the Woman You Love—The Way She Wants You To!* by Kathy Collard Miller and Lucy Sanna. This is one of many books that offer ideas for romancing a woman. Use them for ideas and inspiration, but always customize your romantic gestures to your beloved and what you know she likes and appreciates.

- Lingerie! Sexy and beautiful teddies, silk boxers and other "evening wear," along with some alone time, can make your beloved super-grateful. Enough said.

- Shiva lingam stone! Shiva lingam is an amazing stone that enhances the libido and helps open the sacral chakras. Having clear intentions to expand your sacral energy exchange with one another, you can do the following meditation. Start by sitting in the *yab yum* tantric position: one person sits on the other's lap, legs wrapped around each other; hold the shiva lingam stone together with your hands entwined, foreheads together, matching each other's breath patterns.

Journal on Romance Me

Use this space to leave some notes and suggestions for your beloved of what romance looks and feels like to you.

_____

_____

_____

_____

_____

_____

_____

_____

_____

_____

_____

_____

_____

_____

_____

_____

_____

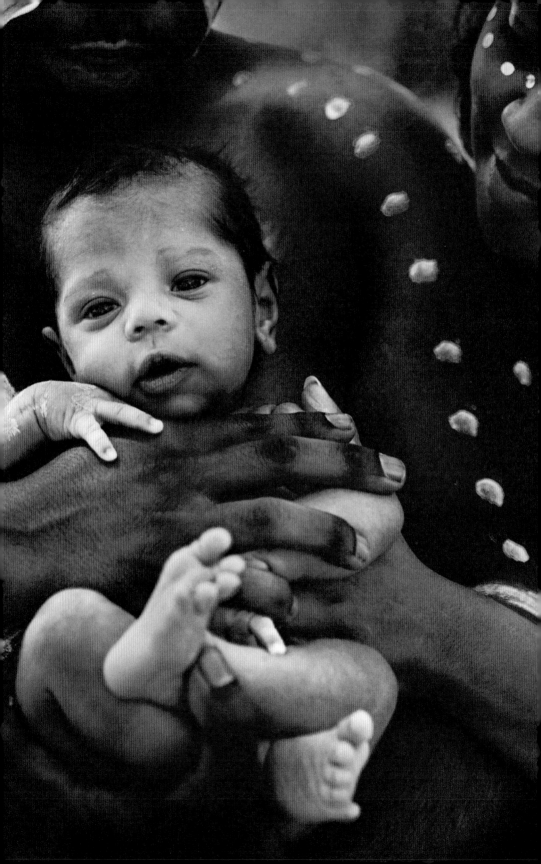

Family Fold

uplift those around you

[Your family is] God's gift

to you, as you are to them.

~DESMOND TUTU

The atmosphere of our lives is characterized by the people who surround us. Our relationships consist of layers of intimacy, beginning with the inner sphere of you and your significant other, and then your immediate family including your children. From there the layers expand to include extended family, close friends, then coworkers, etc.

The core of this book is a focus on your relationship with your spouse, partner, or lover, but the principles outlined here apply to and affect all relationships in your sphere. Bringing a focus on the Sacred to all of these connections will transform your life. You will find that people return your kindness with more kindness, the flow of your day will be easier, and you will be surrounded by smiles all day long. And, as true as this may be, a more profound effect is that you will be acting as an example and a catalyst for others to begin to live in this same way. You will be spreading love, and literally making a positive difference in the world.

YOURSELF

The most profound relationships in your life besides the one with your beloved are with your children. The very best that we can do for our children is for them to feel loved, seen, valued, and respected. When our children embody these high-vibration feelings, they radiate them back to us, making our home a truly wonderful, holy, sacred space. Creating love practices with our children not only helps them feel the love that they need to grow and develop into wonderful human beings, it also teaches them to live in high vibration.

Children are very connected to Source, as they are new to the planet; they carry a fresh and innocent perspective on love, and are naturally present in everything they do. When we pay close attention, they can be teachers as well as students of life. We always strongly recommend that couples take practices home from the live Sacred Relationship retreats and implement them with their children.

The most effective family practices that we have found include creating Sacred Space, gratitude practices, polishing your heart, and teaching them to see beyond a person's negative actions to the pain that lives inside them—essentially empathy. All of these practices, and the feelings and thoughts that they engender, come very naturally to children, so do not be surprised if they eat this stuff up like candy!

THE COUPLE

As you and your beloved begin practicing and living a Sacred Relationship, your children, family, and friends will notice. It is important for you to share with others how you hold your beloved and your children sacred. Express your love in ways that are visible to the world, offering teachable moments to those around you. Involve your children in your family practices, and have them take up some of their own. Share your love, compassion, joy, and empathy for your beloved with your family and friends. Make decisions—and take actions—to give freely to others. All of these practices will increase the quality of your life, and cannot help but inspire those around you.

HEART WORK: *Practice with Your Family*

One of the most transformative practices in difficult relationships comes from the concepts of vibration, compassion, and unconditional love. Our son Bodhi is an especially sensitive soul, and as a young child was easily upset. We learned early on that, when he would begin to act out, admonitions such as "stop teasing your sister" or "don't be sassy," or threatening to take away toys or dessert, did not affect his behavior, and might even cause it to escalate.

Our family completely transformed when we became conscious of the fact that Bodhi was hurting inside and simply reacting to that pain. Now, whenever we see him getting upset, we can ask, "Bodhi, it seems you aren't feeling good inside. What is wrong, and what can we do to help?" The high vibration of this approach immediately shifted the energy, and just asking the question began the healing.

This is the same approach that we have already suggested when your beloved seems upset or down, as it is very effective for anyone. Imagine how wonderfully peaceful your family will be when you all approach each other in this way, as if you were bowing with respect each time you saw one another. Your children learn from you and model their behaviors after you, so help them live from Divine Mind starting at an early age, and you will gift them with spiritual ascension, purpose, and inner joy.

IDEAS AND PRACTICES

Family gratitude practice

Each day we gather with all of our kids at one of the sacred spots in our home, and everyone says one thing that they are grateful for. This is a high priority for us, and on school days even getting to school on time has to wait while we all do this practice. Gratitude is one of the highest-vibration energy emotions, and helps everyone start the day off in a great place.

Children's Sacred Spaces

All of our children have created and maintained their own Sacred Spaces. These are places they can go when they would like some quiet time, and to store their personal sacred artifacts and learn about living in the Beauty Way. We encourage our children to keep their sacred spaces clean, free from dust and old energy, and freshened with flowers or plants.

Polish your heart

Creating "Polish-Your-Heart Love Oil" was discussed in Week 3. This is a practice that can be done with your children. Rubbing the oil on each other's hearts to symbolize love as a regular practice, and extra times when needed, is a powerful connecting ritual for the entire family.

pairings

- Sacred Space décor: small religious or spiritual statues, flowers, crystals, incense, and other special items are great for your children to collect to begin their Sacred Spaces. You can also encourage daily offerings of love to infuse their spaces with their personal high vibes!

- Book: *Sacred Motherhood* by Anni Daulter and Niki Dewart. *Sacred Motherhood* is a book similar to *Sacred Relationship* that takes the reader through a fifty-two week (year-long) journey to help you connect with your children and yourself in more sacred, beautiful ways.

Journal on Family Fold

Use this space to journal about the changes that you see in your family dynamic after beginning these sacred practices with your children.

_____

_____

_____

_____

_____

_____

_____

_____

_____

_____

_____

_____

_____

_____

_____

SECTION FOUR

WE

Vow

LOVE IS COMMITTING

The winds of change may blow new vivid dreams, soft whispers of gentle shifts, or fierce gusts of movement into your lives.

Vow to open your wings and fly to new lands together.

The waves of emotion may wash away past pains, flood your hearts with cleansing truths, or offer a much-needed reverent cleanse.

Vow to stay in the universal flow of your love.

The fires of transformation may beckon you to cast forth the arrow of your love to land on your destiny.

Vow to live your soul contract with your purest intentions.

The mountains of Gaia may charge you with the noble quest of standing tall among the giants of love.

Vow to stay rooted in your love for each other with steady resolve.

The Spirit Divine may sprinkle magic moments upon your love.

Vow to always believe that you are blessed, and that your spirit guides are protecting you.

Spirit Guides

you are supported

I am never alone; my Soul guides
me and my Guardian Angel protects
me. That is teamwork at its best.

~GENEVIEVE GERARD

You have a secret posse of protectors and guides, and whether you know these as your higher self, guardian angels, spirit guides, or the quiet unmistakable whisper of your intuition, you are not alone in your quest for spiritual growth. These invisible friends guide you away from an impending accident, speak to you through your dreams and memories, have known you your whole soul life, and are actively working for your success. They are present even before you are aware of your connection to them. If you are patient, they will introduce themselves to you, and then you will know that you truly are never alone in this life.

YOURSELF

The thing about spiritual growth is that the challenges can be trying; they can demand soul-stretching beyond what you think you can handle. At times you may feel lost, or struggle to see the way through a situation with your highest self still intact. It is in these moments when you can give your struggle up to divine guidance.

You don't need to figure everything out on your own. Lean into your circle of spirit guides, seek their counsel, and take on a new set of eyes. Spirit guides see things in a different way, and communicate with you when you are awake to their subtle bodies. They take a long view over your entire spiritual journey; they see the tender moments, and offer downloads and signs that they are watching. Always and in all ways, they have your best interest at heart.

Have you ever looked at a clock at 11:11 or 12:44, for example? Such synchronicities may be signs from your guides that they are ever-present, watching and offering you their help if you pay close attention. When you first begin working with your guides, you may think that it is just your imagination—but don't let your rational mind limit your experience. Where does your imagination come from? Miracles can only happen in your life if you believe they can.

THE COUPLE

Have you considered what you are here to do as a couple? What is the *spiritual mission* of the two of you together? What will your legacy be?

Working with your collective spirit guides offers you the opportunity to do real growth work together. When you open to divine guidance, your relationship is filled with inspiration and creativity. You begin to weave your soul paths together to do the work you are both meant to do with each other, and then you start to understand your shared vision and limitless potential for intentional loving.

HEART WORK: *Connect with Your Guides*

There are many ways to connect with spirit guides. The most important first step is believing that you have guides who want to work on your behalf, being willing to surrender to this great mystery, and having an open mind and heart. Across all cultures, there are time-tested practices for connecting with these guides. It could be prayer, meditation, oracle cards, or even visualizations. Please explore ways that feel authentic and meaningful for you.

A SIMPLE MEDITATION TO MEET YOUR HIGHER SELF

- Close your eyes, place your bare feet in contact with the Earth, and touch your tongue to the roof of your mouth to complete the energetic circuit in your body.

- Breathe deeply and choose to fully inhabit your body. Take a few minutes to observe how you are feeling right now—physically, emotionally, mentally, and spiritually.

- In your mind's eye, see your grounding cord running from the base of your spine deep into the center of the Earth. Be generous with yourself, and visualize a strong, well-anchored cord. Let your emotions, thoughts, and concerns flow down your cord in a swirling spiral, and be transmuted. Feel the warm, soothing light of the Earth's core flowing up your cord and into your body. This energy coils around your entire energetic grid, balancing, nourishing, and healing all parts of you.

- Now tune in with your sky cord. This cord reaches from the center of your crown far into the heavens. Here you are connected to the heart of the great cosmos. You are perfectly balanced and centered between Heaven and Earth, the child of both. Your energy flows up this cord, communing with stars and sharing information about your journey thus far. This energy is transmuted in the heavens, and infinite love and healing light swirl back down the spiral of your cord and into your whole body. You are innately and divinely connected to all the energy of the universe; you are a small, unique, essential part of this great song of life.

- Take three deep breaths. You are balanced, connected, and in communion with Spirit. In your mind's eye you see a path before you. It is well-worn, familiar, and smoothed by ancient footsteps. Curious, you follow the path into the distance toward a sky filled with infinite stars. The quiet violet light is playing tricks on your eyes, and you can't tell if it is dawn or dusk. It is no time, and any time. It is everywhere, and nowhere.

- You realize after walking a little way that you are already where you need to be, and so you sit. Ever so gently, you begin to float upward. You feel safe and light as you drift toward the heavens.

- Soon you come to a golden platform, suspended in the clouds as if by magic. In front of you is a beautiful temple door with a golden offering bowl outside. You leave a small gift in the bowl as you enter.

- In the center of the temple a labyrinth is laid out on the floor, lit by candles and oil lamps. You slowly begin to walk the labyrinth, coiling carefully into its glorious center. Once there, know that you are connected with the benevolent loving spirit of your higher self, and that this guide has only your best and highest good in mind.

- Take a moment to ask for divine guidance here in this perfect moment. Know that Spirit sees and knows you in this sacred place.
- When you are ready, trace your steps back out of the labyrinth. When you leave the temple, you find a golden elevator leading back down to the path. Walk the path back to your starting place. Focus once more on your breath and your contact with the Earth.
- Open your eyes, and allow pure love to fill all parts of you. Smile with soft contentment and peace.
- Stay in this place as long as you like. You may choose to close the practice with a heart smile and a deep breath. Take time to journal and reflect afterward.

IDEAS AND PRACTICES

See below for how to make and use a wonderful "Spirit-Anointing Oil" to help you connect to your spirit guides.

SPIRIT-ANOINTING OIL

- ⅓ ounce pure oil (olive or coconut works fine)
- 8 drops geranium essential oil
- 7 drops vervain essential oil
- 3 drops sandalwood essential oil
- 3 drops lotus flower essence
- 1 spiral or labyrinth, drawn on a piece of paper
- 1 white seven-day jar candle
- 1 black seven-day jar candle

Combine all your ingredients in a beautiful vessel. Place it in the center of the spiral or labyrinth, setting the small candles on either side to represent the yin and the yang, the light and the mystery.

Light the candles, and invoke Spirit. Ask the Divine to infuse into your oil.

Once the candles have burned down, and you feel your oil is ready, decant it into a small container.

Anoint your crown, your third eye, and anywhere else down your centerline in preparation for meditation or journeywork with your spirit guides.

pairings

- Oracle deck: *Sacred Rebels Oracle: Guidance for Living a Unique and Authentic Life* by Alana Fairchild. This is a wonderful deck for accessing guidance from the higher realms.

- Card deck: *The Wild Unknown Animal Spirit Deck* by Kim Krans. This is a wonderful deck for connecting with your animal spirit guides, asking them for daily guidance, and learning from their innate medicine.

- Crystal: apophyllite. Apophyllite is a light, shining crystal of very high vibration. It helps to bring contact with your truest self, and to see across dimensions and planes of reality, so it is especially helpful for meditation and journeywork. This crystal goes beyond simply supporting the practice of meditation and journeywork; it also nurtures your ability to bring the insights you gain into the present moment.

Journal on Spirit Guides

Use this space to journal about your
connection to your spirit guides, and
what new insights they are sharing with
you. List who your spirit guides are, if you
have been introduced, and reflect on your
shared grand purpose as a couple.

_____

_____

_____

_____

_____

_____

_____

_____

_____

_____

_____

_____

_____

_____

_____

_____

Spiritual Mind

living with purpose

The answers you seek will never
come when the mind is busy;
they come when the mind is still.

~UNKNOWN

Understanding your spirit path will help you reshape your relationship and elevate it to Sacred. Learning ways to tap into your higher consciousness will root you in confidence about the choices and directions you take personally and with your beloved. Take a walk in the fields of divinity, and you will bring more peace to your heart and mind.

YOURSELF

Spiritual mind is how you relate to your higher self, mastering the ability to quiet your mind in order to listen to your spirit guides. As you move into infusing your relationship with fresh vows, it is more important than ever that you enter into those commitments with full awareness. This can only happen if you are in tune with your spiritual mind and have begun to align your thoughts with your new path.

The universe provides assistance in these matters if you invite that guidance, quiet your mind, and listen to the answers provided. Everyone seeks to understand their higher purpose in life, and being able to tap into your spiritual awareness will help you to understand and learn from every lesson that is presented to you.

THE COUPLE

What is your spiritual health as a couple? Do you believe you are growing together in your quest for purpose, or starting to walk down separate paths? Understanding the bigger picture, your journey together, and how you relate spiritually as a couple is part of figuring out the mystery of your soul contract with each other. You may have come together to create special little humans who will help heal the world, or to build a business, or to help one another grow into your full individual potential. If you feel unmatched in this way, spending time in spiritual mind where you are open to receiving information and guidance can help you to drop into a place of unfolding how the two of you can meet more in the middle.

HEART WORK: *Understanding Living with Purpose*

Every decision you make in life is just a choice. Because humanity has been blessed with free will, you can exercise this right by living with purpose. When you choose this purpose as a life path, you elevate the mundane to Sacred, and understand that every moment you are alive is a breathing meditation.

When you feel numb, stuck, scared, separate, depressed, anxious, or immobile, you cut yourself off from moving through the world armed with sacred purpose and tapped into conscious awareness. Being awake in life, by contrast, is a place of beauty, connection, destiny, magic, and spiritual presence.

Which do you choose?

IDEAS AND PRACTICES

You can make a simple choice to live your life with purpose; this will give Spirit the permission to guide you in right action to where you need to be. The Bright Light Meditation and Spirit-Path Card Readings (see below) can help you open up to inner guidance about your spiritual purpose.

BRIGHT LIGHT MEDITATION

For this exercise, we suggest that you begin by setting up a sacred circle to sit in, creating a layer of psychic protection as you move deep within yourself.

- Sit in a comfortable position, and bring your focus to the here and now with a few deep, cleansing breaths.

- Visualize a ball of bright, beautiful light, like a little sun, located in a spot about eighteen inches directly above the top of your head (known as the eighth chakra) where your physical being connects with your higher self. Next, ask your spirit guides for the gift of the frequencies of light that will bring you insight, high-vibration energy, and answers to your spiritual questions.

- Move your focus to your heart (fourth chakra) and hold a deep sense and feeling of gratitude while the energy is downloaded into your heart—fifteen to thirty seconds or more, until the process feels complete—allowing this process to organically unfold.

- When you are ready, take several deep breaths. With each outbreath, focus on moving the energy from your heart to every part of your body, feeding each cell with the light containing your gift. Make sure that you hold a strong intention to integrate these new energies into your body.

- Journal about any information that comes to you.

SPIRIT-PATH CARD READING

Once you are open to the light frequencies and information, do a spirit path reading. We recommend using the *Sacred Path Cards* by Jamie Sams for this quest, but any intuitive cards you are drawn to will serve you well.

- Sit in your sacred circle, and center yourself by feeling the Earth beneath you. Ask your spirit guides to help you to choose the appropriate cards from whatever deck you have decided to use. Trust that you have the innate wisdom to interpret the cards correctly in order to apply their messages to your life.

- To perform the reading, shuffle and mix the cards well. As you are doing this, hold the intention to draw the specific cards that will help you to learn and grow.

- Place the cards face down, and fan them out. Then hold your hand above the cards, and feel your way to the correct card. In this part of the exercise, get out of your head and into your feeling body as much as possible.

- Choose your cards according to any particular spread in the book that may call to you.
- Scribe any insights you glean from this process.

pairings

- Card deck: *Sacred Path Cards* by Jamie Sams. This is a divination deck to help seekers along their spiritual paths. It offers deep insights into finding your life purpose while being guided by your higher-consciousness self. The deck comes with a book offering avenues to readings that are accessible even for the novice.

- White sage for smudging. Use a white sage bundle to clear your energy, raise your vibration, and step into your spirit mind more easily. Take a smudging bundle, light it, and allow the sage smoke to wash over your body and clean your energy field until you feel your vibration rise.

Journal on Spiritual Mind

Use this space to journal about the results of your meditation and Spirit-Path Card Reading.

_____

_____

_____

_____

_____

_____

_____

_____

_____

_____

_____

_____

_____

_____

_____

_____

Removing Fair

tit for tat makes your relationship fall flat

What's fair ain't necessarily right.

~TONI MORRISON,
Beloved

One of the themes throughout this book is that true love is selfless giving. When you start worrying about whether you are getting equal to what you are giving, ego and self-centeredness come into play, and will pollute your relationship with low-vibration energy.

YOURSELF

At a Sacred Relationship live retreat, we met a couple—call them Charlie and Maria—who were in a pretty bad place. They had been together twenty years, since high school, and there had been an affair early in their relationship that had created a Grand Canyon-sized gulf between them. Maria demanded that Charlie change and start doing the things that she wanted, and Charlie wanted a guarantee in return that, if he started doing them, the relationship would be healed and Maria would stay with him. Charlie also wanted the deep wound of the affair to be gone.

For two solid days, they were at an impasse, completely focused on wanting the other to make the first gesture and take the first step. We kept redirecting them to the necessity of trust, and having the courage to take the first step—to be the one who gives freely without expectation of return.

Charlie finally decided that he was willing to take the first step, drop his ego, and be all-in, and was finally able to begin the work wholeheartedly. It could have been Maria who jumped off that ego-cliff into the arms of unconditional love, but one of them had to break the impasse, see beyond past frustrations, hurts, and wounds, and say YES to the relationship. This allowed them to take the next steps as a couple toward bringing understanding and joy back into their relationship.

Being willing to give and to love without requiring an equal exchange is an act of spiritual mastery and serves your highest good. The difference between an attitude of "I'll only do this if you do that first" and an attitude of unconditional love is an entire world of potential healing—one you want to make sure you are in right relationship with. Be willing to take a first step in faith every time; do it just because you love your partner, because you want them to be happy, and because you want to heal your relationship. In return, you will be filled with joy and love, and your heart will heal as the positive energy between you grows.

THE COUPLE

Keeping score sucks the positive juju out of your relationship. When you get to the point where you are mad because you washed the dishes, changed the oil in the car, and made the kids' lunches when your partner only went grocery shopping, then you have to admit that the romance has been replaced by frustration, competition, and ego.

Arguing about who's not doing enough signals that it's time to take a step back and re-examine everyone's attitude toward the work of supporting your family. It is fine to have discussions about equitable and appropriate sharing of family duties, but it must always be done in high vibration, love, and care. Stay far away from keeping score with one another, even just in your mind, as it inevitably ends nowhere pleasant and, in the end, does not serve the highest good for either of you.

HEART WORK: *Stay in High Vibration*

The heart work of "removing fair" is about dropping ego and resistance. Be present in whatever you are doing and whatever situation you are in. Develop a gratitude practice to counteract the low vibrations of frustration or fear whenever you feel you are being asked to contribute or risk more than your beloved. Focus on all of the wonderful things in the situation that you can be grateful for, rather than what you believe you are not getting equally for yourself.

Every situation, circumstance, or conflict is an opportunity to choose to respond either in high vibration or low vibration. Every time you choose high vibration, you expand in happiness, peace, and joy. Every time you recognize the abundance in your life, and feel and express gratitude, you are attracting even more gold into your life.

Why would you want to give away your power to become happier and more abundant by deciding to only live in high vibration if your beloved does it first? You are, always and in all ways, in control of how you map your life, so choose to be your best self regardless of any circumstance around you—and see how that decision shifts your whole experience of life.

IDEAS AND PRACTICES

We talk a lot about gratitude practices in this book because gratitude is the foundation of your spiritual growth. And because there are many ways to color your picture of gratitude in your life, we want to give you several options. One is the Gratitude Practice (see below).

GRATITUDE PRACTICE

Create the habit of moving to a place of gratitude every time you begin to feel in resistance to something. Resistance can manifest in many ways—anger, frustration, negative inner dialogue, sorrow, wishing things were different, etc. When you notice these, begin to focus on aspects of the situation that you are grateful for. There is so much in our lives that we take for granted that there are always many gifts you can recognize at any time, for instance:

- I am grateful that I have two hands to wash the dishes.

- I am grateful that I have two legs to walk across the room.

- I am grateful that I have a wonderful family to serve.

- I am grateful that I am having this opportunity to choose a higher-vibration response.

Gratitude is such a high-vibration state of being that injecting it into your day as much as possible is like taking a turbo-charged rocket to feeling better.

I will go first!

This practice helps you break out of a situation where you and your beloved are arguing tit-for-tat on who needs to move into high vibration first. Simply decide that you will always be the one to go first. This may take some practice in letting go of your ego, but instead of thinking of it as admitting defeat, think of it as demonstrating your courage, strength, and high vibration.

When you are in an argument, be the first to step back and say, "Whatever our disagreement, I will yield because I love you, and because it is more important for our relationship to be in high vibration than to be engaged in this argument." When there is a disagreement over who should do something, be the first to say, "I will take up this work as a service to you, because you are my love and I want to be in service to you."

Be the change that you want to see in your relationship; be proactive, and be a leader. You are the one who will benefit most by raising your own vibration and shifting the dynamic of your connection with your beloved.

pairings

- Mantra: *"I feed my relationship, not my ego."* Use this mantra with a mala, or train yourself to revisit it anytime you get into conflict with your beloved. Say this mantra several times throughout the day and use it as a touchstone to stay in high vibration.

- Song: "Down to the River to Pray" by Alison Krauss. This beautiful tune reminds you to stay connected to Spirit and your highest self through all the struggles that may bring you suffering.

RIVER STONE BALANCE MEDITATION

The stones have no quarrel with you, and want to teach and guide you into balance.

- Go down to a riverbank, beach, or other nature spot and find some stones that call to you.

- Sit with the stone people for a while, and ask them to help bring you into balance; then place one stone on top of another, stacking them until they are fully balanced on each other.

- After you are finished, sit in silence and gratitude for the teachings and blessings you received from nature.

Journal on Removing Fair

Sketch a picture in this space that represents yourself, your beloved, and the negativity between you when you are in disagreement. Then draw another picture without the negativity. Notice the feelings that the new picture brings up in you, and journal about what YOU are willing to do to bring those feelings into your experience.

Love Mandala

prayer for us

Each person's life is like a mandala—
a vast, limitless circle. We stand in
the center of our own circle, and
everything we see, hear, and think
forms the mandala of our life.

~PEMA CHÖDRÖN

In Tibetan culture, sand mandalas are prepared to honor deities, send prayers for all into the universe, and provide a lesson on impermanence. There are so many teachings to be gathered at the center of a mandala prayer, as if it called and we followed.

Maintaining a Sacred Relationship does take heart work, daily practices, dedication, love, compassion, joy, and empathy, but it also takes some good old-fashioned prayers. Tapping the shoulders of spirit guides to help usher you down your personal path is one form of prayer, and sending vibrational medicine and healing to your relationship through the creation of a mandala is another.

A mandala is a meditative geometric design with a core center in which a primary deity or blessing lives, and its soul purpose is to use its vibrational medicine to help heal others and the world. These very delicate and intricate designs are carefully crafted as purification palaces for housing the most precious thoughts, energies, prayers, and intentions.

In order to construct a love mandala that speaks to the many layers of your connection with your beloved, the span of your relationship life deserves a look into all the rich patterns, shapes, and teachings that live and breathe within its chambers—after which a carefully constructed physical prayer can be beautifully made and then, in true Tibetan tradition, swept away to amplify its impermanence.

YOURSELF

Living in the flow of the universe is how you relieve the heaviness of life. Have you ever heard a call from the Divine that you were meant to go somewhere, or do or create something, and you did not follow it? Have you had a deep inner knowing that you were meant to do something else with your life, but felt too afraid to pursue your real heart's dream? To put it into this century's context, it's like deleting a text message from your guru, or God, or your spiritual master—not a good idea! That call puts you into the flow of your destiny, and when you answer it you will witness the universe configuring itself to make it happen.

Many people do not trust these calls, and they struggle with living from a sense of lack, as if there won't be enough abundance to care for them should they follow the dream in their hearts. The universal plan is bigger than our awareness, and we are humbled to be one of its moving parts. If you live in the flow and answer your heart calls, you will see how the elements of the universe will fall into place at the right moments for your destiny to play out.

THE COUPLE

Sending energy out into the universe on behalf of your relationship is an act of hope and a call for support. Taking it to a sacred level by utilizing the mandala as an outlet to share this prayer with others is compassionate generosity, and leaves Beauty-Way energy behind, both to infuse your love and to help heal the world.

We humans suffer because we live in expectation and attachment; we overspend our emotional currency on salty exchanges and anger, and leave little room to elevate the mundane moments to sacred. Take time as a couple to look at the core beauty of your relationship, its soul purpose, and place it in the center of your figurative palace.

After doing this, each of you spend time crafting prayers for your love that will uplift, support, energize, and elevate your relationship. Write these down, and then meditate together on elevating your connection to a sacred level and really seeing what that looks like on a daily basis. Send prayers into the universe for your love and the love of others.

HEART WORK: *Understanding Impermanence*

Suffering dwells in the house of attachment, so if you can understand the concept of impermanence and embrace its gifts, you will suffer less. The only true constant is change, and if you struggle with this as reality, much of your life is spent swimming upstream.

When the Tibetans create the masterful, intricate sand prayers of a mandala manifestation, they chant while they are doing it, infusing the mandala with the highest vibrations. When this sacred ritual is completed, they sweep the sand away into the rivers, into an ever-changing, flowing body of water, in order to send the prayers into the world for others. They are not attached to their hard work because they spent days creating it; rather, they affirm that it served out its purpose in that form and must transition into new a form to complete its larger purpose.

Relationships are similar, in that they consistently move and shape-shift. When we resist this natural flow, we both suffer. To understand impermanence is to embrace the laws of nature and to see your part in the dance of life. Do not stay stagnant, because you will wither away; instead, live deeply in the flow, listen to where you are called, pray, bow, and give to others freely. You will always be where you are meant to be.

IDEAS AND PRACTICES

As you and your beloved are working together to create your Sacred Relationship, a beautiful practice is to create art together that represents your vision of your love and your relationship.

A mandala in both Buddhist and Hindu spirituality is a geometric figure representing the entire universe. In our practices we refer to a love mandala as a geometric figure representing the wholeness of your relationship with your beloved, created by you together in love and harmony.

Step-by-step instructions for creating a love mandala with your beloved are desribed in "Create a Love Mandala" below.

CREATE A LOVE MANDALA

At the Sacred Relationship live retreats, couples create a healing flower mandala as a sacred prayer to the universe on behalf of their great love story. They are given many different types of deconstructed flowers, again emphasizing impermanence— once it was a blossoming flower on a path, and now it becomes the petals of a prayer. The couples are charged with the task of collectively creating a beautiful design that reflects their love story. Then they send their prayers out into the universe, and immediately sweep their mandala away.

- First, both of you write your prayers for your relationship—see "The Couple," above.

- Gather flowers from your garden, or just nature items from outside your home.

- Sit together and use these items to start creating a masterful design on the ground with precision and care. Remember that mandalas are geometrically shaped, with one core center purpose as the jewel in the crown. Take your time and make it beautiful, playing high-vibration music as you create.

- When you have completed the mandala, light candles around it and come together to say the prayers that you wrote down earlier.

- Once your prayers have been heard, ask the winds of impermanence and change to sweep them away so that their seeds can land on others less fortunate who are in need of healing and compassion.

- Sweep your mandala away so it can finish fulfilling its work.

pairings

- Mandala coloring books. There is a new trend of adult-style coloring books being used as a meditative practice, and there are several mandala versions of those. The peaceful practice of coloring a mandala can bring about a calming state of mind, a relaxed body, and a recharged spirit.

- Crystal: fluorite. Fluorite is a beautiful stone that helps you connect to intuition and universal flow. If you are a rigid person, resisting change and living very tightly wound, pick up a piece of fluorite. You can keep this crystal in a pocket or on a simple necklace, where the crystal stays close to the heart chakra and will work as a solid reminder to stay in the flow of your life.

Journal on Love Mandala

Use this space to write about how you feel
about impermanence, and make note
of your prayers for your relationship.
Logging them here will give you a
reference point to return to as needed.

_____

_____

_____

_____

_____

_____

_____

_____

_____

_____

_____

_____

_____

_____

_____

_____

_____

Sacred Agreements

what are you willing to do?

An agreement cannot be
the result of an imposition.

~NESTOR KIRCHNER

The suggestions and approaches that we recommend in this book require you to make and keep agreements. These are Sacred Agreements to think and act in new ways that will lead you to the euphoric and uplifted feelings of peace, joy, happiness, and fulfillment that come from living in a Sacred Relationship. However, we have seen time and time again in our work with couples that no one can be forced or pushed into practices. True and lasting change will only come when you are ready, committed, and motivated to step into a new way of being.

YOURSELF

Alive in you, all of the wisdom, insight, and knowledge you need to live in Sacred Relationship with your beloved already exists. However, you may have forgotten and lost touch with this wisdom. The purpose of the teachings presented in this book and in our retreats is to awaken your connection to this knowledge, so that remembering your true nature is as easy as a walk in the park.

This means taking a deep drink of who you really are, what you came here to accomplish in this lifetime, and your personal medicine gifts, and learning how to live in deep gratitude, peace, joy, and happiness. It is this remembering that provides the desire and motivation to change your life.

All of the low-vibration habits and reactions that you carry within you are either coping mechanisms that you have developed to deal with hurt and pain, or responses that have been taught to you as acceptable ways to fit in with society. Either way, they were originally there to protect and support you at certain times in your life development. As you embrace the true nature of who you are, however, those old ways only hold you back from moving onward and upward. The fact that you are reading this book is proof that you are ready and have the ability to shed the old robes of low vibration and cloak yourself with peace, joy, and fulfillment.

THE COUPLE

As you embark upon your Sacred Relationship, you are making the basic agreements to 1) raise your own personal vibration and 2) feed high-vibration energy to your beloved. These two agreements go hand in hand, and each one requires and works in concert with the other. To support your fulfilling these, you will be making additional agreements to take up practices that support living in high vibration for both you and your beloved.

This is where the rubber meets the road. Holding these agreements sacred and prioritizing them above the mundane habits where you spend much of your time each day is critically important. Every low-vibration story that you leave behind, and every new habit that you create, represents a huge energetic shift in your life. Do not underestimate this power.

Deep, internal shifting of ingrained patterns is not easy, and requires that you look profoundly into what patterns you want to drop, and understand the role they have played in your life. Why did these habits that do not serve your highest good form to begin with? Why have you continued practicing them? How have they seemingly supported some aspects in you? How have they limited you?

You must see them clearly, with fresh eyes, in order to truly become motivated to drop them. In the same way, we encourage you to look at the new practices and ask the same questions: why are you taking up these particular practices? How do you see them helping you, and how will they support you? Clear and accurate understanding of these things will help you keep your Sacred Agreements with yourself and with your beloved.

HEART WORK: *Be All In*

Sometimes low-vibration habits are highly addictive, and frankly tough to kick. Alcohol is one of the most common addictions that we see, but we have also worked with folks addicted to video games, marijuana, pornography, sugar, flirting/communicating with exes, and a whole slew of other things that do not serve the highest good. Some of our Sacred Relationship Retreat participants are able to make immediate and sustained changes based on an awakening they have during our shared time together.

We had one young man who spent upwards of ten hours per day playing video games. At the retreat he had a complete epiphany, and suddenly it was very clear to him how that amount of time and energy going into a low-vibration pastime was negatively affecting his relationship and risking his relationship with his family. He did some powerful release work at the retreat, went home, and threw out his gaming gear—and he has not touched it in the several years since.

However, we have also had cases where participants are less sure about their desire to give up old, toxic habits. We know several people who drink to excess on a regular basis, and fail to see how this behavior negatively affects their connections with their spouses. There have been times at the Sacred Relationship Retreats when one person would threaten to leave the relationship if the drinking did not end. However, keep in mind that changes or agreements made under threat are often short-lived, or result in many regressions.

Internal changes to uproot addictions are tough, and need regular support, sometimes professional help, and mostly an internal awakening to really see the low-vibration effects. The sacredness of a retreat can be the impetus to that awakening, and can allow the individual to see the path to hope with new eyes, and to desire a way out of the darkness. Even addictions are choices you make—otherwise no one would ever be able to kick them to the curb—but to cleanse yourself of toxic junk really takes internal resolve, discipline, action, compassion, and insight. There is no more important exercise than to see clearly what behaviors you choose to practice, and understand the effects they can have on creating the life you want.

IDEAS AND PRACTICES

Create a vision board

When working to release old, limiting habits and create new, supportive ones, it is helpful to keep presence in your heart and your goals fresh in Beginner's Mind. Creating a vision board can be a great visual to keep these practices current in your daily life.

Begin with a large poster board, and in the center create a visual artistic representation of the life and relationship that you want. You can draw, paint, or collage using images from magazines, Pinterest, or other resources. Then, circling around the center, add visual images of all of the positive practices you are taking up to create your vision.

Loss of old habits must be represented by positive images. For example, if you are letting go of alcohol, don't show a picture of a martini with a big red X through it—rather, use images that represent sobriety, purification, health, etc.

Once you have created the board, hang it in a location where you will see it every day. Make a point to stop and look at it, and remind yourself of what you want and the agreements that you have made with yourself and your beloved. Visual reminders go a long way in helping you stay grounded in your resolve for change.

pairings

- Book: *The Art of Communicating* by Thich Nhat Hanh. This great, practical book is very short and easy to read. It contains useful Buddhist mindfulness practices to help keep you focused on raising your vibration through the act of loving kindness and heartfelt communication. Thich Nhat Hanh is a guru of Anni's, and his work has provided deep insights into living a compassionate life.

- Crystal: red calcite. This crystal is wonderful for preventing negative patterns. Keep a piece under your pillow at night so that the subtle energy of the crystal can seep into your unconscious mind and start to live in your awareness during the daylight hours. If you are really struggling with addiction, keep a piece in your pocket and hold it when you need to, allowing it to be a touchstone for remembrance of your true nature.

Journal on Sacred Agreements

Use this space to list low-vibration habits
that you are committing to release.
Journal here about where they came from,
why you have held on to them, and how
letting them go will benefit your life.

_____

_____

_____

_____

_____

_____

_____

_____

_____

_____

_____

_____

_____

_____

Salt Bowl Intentions

calling it in

The cure for anything is
saltwater: sweat, tears, or the sea.

~ISAK DINESEN

Salt has long been used for folk magic. It is said that the crystals of salt hold memory, and it is this power that allows salt to work as an ancient tool for binding your word with your intentions. An old world tradition is that you would bind a contract or vow by putting a pinch of salt into the other's satchel, and you were only allowed to break your vow if you could take back every grain.

Salt also has protective powers, preserving the integrity of your word and intention when you bring them together. Like all acts of prayer and magic, the most powerful work is accomplished when you unite your purest, most heartfelt will with action.

Now is the time to let go and believe in magic. Open to the Great Mystery that you don't know anything except the present moment, which means that anything could happen in the next moment. Salt Bowl Intentions are the sweet seeds of hope, whispered, hidden dreams, and tear-scented words of the heart, witnessed and shared so that they may take hold and flourish for the greater good of all.

Now is the time to call in the magic and the wonder. Call in your purest intentions in word, thought, and deed.

YOURSELF

Sacred Salt Bowls are a signature ritual that we use to end all of our Sacred Living Movement live retreats. You put your purest intentions, represented by some natural herb or essential oil, for example, into a bowl of clean salt, and this gets mixed in with everyone else's items and intentions. Then the Mother Salt is added, which is a combination of all the salts ever created by all the people who have ever attended a Sacred Living Retreat.

These Mother Salts are very valuable and sacred, as they contain the magical intentions of thousands of people and their wishes, hopes, and dreams. They came from all over the world, and have touched many shores and forests. This is now being offered to you as a ritual to bring forth your hopes, lay them bare, and surrender to a little bit of magic!

As you prepare for this ceremony, reflect back on all the work you have done on yourself as a spiritual being, all the layers you have shed and the stories you have reshaped. Consider for a moment what seeds you are planting for the future. In what areas do you need a little extra help and universal support? If you lived with no limits on your love or your life, what would that look like? If you could ask for anything to help you create that vision, what would it be?

THE COUPLE

Your relationship is a precious plant that needs to be watered, nourished, and cared for by both of you in order to survive. Salt Bowl intentions are part of the sustenance you are committing to. Your wishes, hopes, and needs are poured into the fertile, primordial cauldron of the universe so that they may take root in your lives.

The heart work you have done needs to stay strong, your practices need to maintain their purity, and your commitment to living a sacred life with each other must be unwavering. Ask yourselves as a couple: what would it look like if there were no limits on your love and in your life? If both of you could ask for anything to help you create that vision, what would it be?

HEART WORK: *Focusing Pure Intention*

The purpose of ritual is to perform physical and mental practices that reinforce and deepen intentions held in your mind. Cleansing and purification are common and important practices often performed prior to ritual—or as rituals themselves—to let go of low-vibration thoughts and energies. Please see "Sacred Bathing" below for one suggested cleansing practice.

Before you hold any ceremony, it is good to prepare yourself physically and spiritually. A traditional way to do this is through Sacred Bathing.

- This bath or shower is done with specific intention and the support of added herbs such as rosemary, flower essences such as yarrow, and crystals such as clear quartz. But you can use whatever you have on hand to support your intention. Don't be worried about having special tools—magic happens in everyday life, with simple things, and ceremony comes from inside. The intention here is to wash away any negative energy that you may have picked up or had dumped on you, that has stuck to your auric field like cat hair on a favorite coat. Sacred Bathing can also help you cleanse responsibility for any negative energy that you may have left with someone else. This kind of cleaning feels light, and taps into your spiritual integrity.

- As you soak in the tub or the shower, breathe deeply and really connect with this body you have. Be in your body, wholly and completely. Set your clear intention to clean and clear it on all levels. You can ask for guidance from your helpful healing guides, spirits, angels, power animals, or whomever you usually pray to.

- As you soak, feel the herbs helping you to gently release with love and kindness any energy that doesn't belong to you or serve you in your highest good. You may even want to say out loud that you are releasing any energy that does not belong to you. Be gentle but firm. Don't judge any images that pop into your head—just let them go, like little bubbles bursting into light.

- Now take a few minutes to enjoy this light feeling. Breathe deeply, and stay connected to your body. It is now time to call back your own positive energy. Feel it spooling into you, refilling your inner sparkle and light. With kindness and love, allow yourself to be whole, your spirit and body connected. You may even want to say out loud: "I call back all of my positive energy with love and kindness." Be gentle but firm—you need to mean it. Again, don't judge yourself or any images or feelings that come up. This is just energy—it's not good or bad.

- Allow yourself to enjoy the newly refreshed, positive space of love that you have created around and within you.

IDEAS AND PRACTICES

Going to the bowl

Going to the bowl is a magical and time-honored Sacred Living Movement tradition. You can set this up as an intimate ceremony for yourself and your beloved, or include your whole family if you like. Create your own Mother Salt to put in future Salt Bowls (see "Salt Bowl Ceremony" below).

THE SALT BOWL CEREMONY

1. Place a selection of items such as flower essences, dried herbs, flowers, spices, crystal beads, crystals, essential oils, and edible glitter in the center of the circle.

2. Choose a large, beautiful bowl, cleanse it with the smoke of white sage, and fill it with fine sea salt. Place this in the center of the circle as well.

3. Sit around the bowl with your beloved and begin talking about what each of you needs as an individual right now, and what you need as a couple. This is the time to talk about dreams, ask for inspiration, and create hope and possibility. Let a bubble of these pure intentions form around you both.

4. When you are ready, each of you chooses something to put into the bowl. Take turns putting items into the bowl, saying out loud how that specific ingredient adds your intentions into this bowl of pure manifestation. For example, I sat in circle with a couple once, where a gentleman added some ocean water to remind himself to stay in the flow, and another woman added cacao powder to raise her love level and encourage more sexy time in the bedroom. So add your ingredient, along with your wish of what you want to bring into your life, saying why that ingredient will help your intentions fly free into the universe.

5. Mix your ingredient in with your hands until it is well combined.

6. Go around the circle as many times as you want, making sure to get every last wish into the bowl.

7. When you are finished, place one hand in the bowl and connect with each other through eye contact. Smile and say together, "By the power of three times three, as we will it, so shall it be!" This chant charges up the intentions and sends them out into the universe to work their magic.

8. Transfer your magic salt into a lovely jar, and add a few pinches to your bath or shower as needed. When you refresh it with the next ceremony, keep a spoonful or two to add to the following bowl in order to keep the magic of the Sacred Salt Bowl connected and flowing.

pairings

- Resource: Mountain Rose Herbs. This is a wonderful place to purchase herbs, essences, and essential oils for use in the Salt Bowl.

- Fine sea salt is our favorite salt for use in Salt Bowls, and can be purchased at any grocery store.

- Thrift-store pottery. Perhaps you and your beloved can go thrifting together at local secondhand shops to find a magic Salt Bowl to contain your intentions with beauty and positive energy. Be sure to use white sage smoke to cleanse the bowl before using it for ceremony.

Journal on Salt Bowl Intentions

Use this space to journal about magic, wonder, and the powerful things you are calling into your life. What were your individual and collective sacred Salt Bowl wishes and intentions?

_____

_____

_____

_____

_____

_____

_____

_____

_____

_____

_____

_____

_____

_____

_____

_____

_____

Beauty Way Ceremony

seal the bond

You don't find love, it finds you.
It's got a little bit to do with destiny,
fate, and what's written in the stars.

~ANAÏS NIN

Get in the way of beauty, and let her smack you right in the face with her glorious attitude and unshakable, bright, and shiny energy—it's time to celebrate! If you have done the heart work in this book, and started elevating your relationship to the next level, it's time to mark those accomplishments with ceremony and ritual.

A recommitment ceremony might be just the thing you need to seal the bond between you as you embark on living out your Sacred Relationship. You may decide this should just be a small intimate ceremony for the two of you, or you may choose a more elaborate event, inviting others to the party! The point of this ceremony is to rewrite sacred vows to each other based on your dedication to the practices and to living in high vibration and intentional, conscious loving with your beloved.

YOURSELF

Give yourself a little outbreath of space to really reflect on all the work you have done to do better and be better, to live more in the flow of your life, bow in reverence to love, live from compassion and empathy, and practice Divine Mind. Honor those accomplishments with a full heart, and ask yourself if you are ready to do a recommitment ceremony with your beloved. If the answer is yes, get planning!

Think about standing in front of your beloved, raw and kissed with truth on your lips, sharing deep exchanges of love and tender looks. What do you want to say to your beloved in this ceremonious way? What vows will you make? What beauty can you bring to your circle of love to mark your transition into life as a Sacred Couple?

THE COUPLE

In reading this book and incorporating these ideas into your daily living as a couple, you have been gifted with new life and reshaped ideas about what relationships can strive to become. This is a new path that you are walking, with refreshed dreams, hot new date nights, and mindful care of your well-crafted love—and it deserves celebration.

You are cleansed, pure, and ready to live in intentional love with each other, and this rite of passage may hold more significance than any other ceremonies the two of you may have shared in the past. Whether you do it by yourselves or invite a few special people to bear witness to your love, ritual is needed to mark a new beginning.

HEART WORK: *Rewriting Sacred Vows*

When you first come together with your beloved, you make promises and declarations to each other on a regular basis because is love is the food you eat and the air you breathe. The thing is, though, that these actions are not always taken with consciousness and intentional focus and purpose. They are typically made in the lustful days where you see each other as walking on water, and it's easy to make such dedications and to wax poetic at the drop of a hat.

Creating sacred vows in mindfulness and with heart-work dedications, on the other hand, is in a whole other league, elevated from the newness of the early days to really knowing and speaking to each other's needs and love languages. As you prepare for your recommitment ceremony, each of you can take the time to write vows that stream from your Divine Mind and are truly alive in you. Write them on beautiful paper so that they can become a treasured keepsake in years to come.

IDEAS AND PRACTICES

Recommitment ceremony

At the Sacred Relationship live retreats, we host a recommitment ceremony for the couples on the last day. Every couple dresses in their whites, has sacred vows at the ready, and is willing to step into the flower-petal circle in perfect love and perfect trust.

We start by cleansing the couples with sage and palo santo, and facilitate a Tibetan singing bowl sound-cleanse. After this, each couple steps wholeheartedly into the circle, expressing their love and reading their vows to each other. They exchange new or cleansed rings to seal their bond, and offer each other a necklace that signifies the never-ending circular energy between them. They then share a sacred kiss, receive blessings, and have a slow dance to a signature song that speaks to their love.

This is a lovely ceremony you can adopt as your own, or you can create a special intimate ritual for the two of you to share. This is a Beauty-Way event to really celebrate all the work you two have done, and to mark your commitments with vows and a sacred call to the universe to hold you true to your word.

pairings

- Pick a heart song. As you have grown over time with your beloved—and hopefully since you have been using this book!—the poetry that reflects your love may need refreshing. When you are designing your ceremony, add a slow dance at the end to seal the bond, and choose a song that will speak to your refreshed vows. Some favorites include:
  - Ellie Goulding, "How Long Will I Love You?"
  - Adele, "Make You Feel My Love"
  - James Morrison, "Right By Your Side"
  - Ed Sheeran, "Thinking Out Loud"
  - Van Morrison, "Sweet Thing"
- Sacred singing bowl. Tibetan singing bowls are a spiritual tool used to conjure up mystical harmonic hums, often used in ceremony and ritual. Singing bowls add a sacred touch to your recommitment ceremony and can be used for sound-cleansing each other before sharing vows. You can get singing bowls online or at a New-Age shop.

Journal on Beauty Way Ceremony

Use this space to plan your recommitment ceremony. Scribble ideas and make special plans for how to do your ceremony in the Beauty Way and to make it as special as it can possibly be!

_____

_____

_____

_____

_____

_____

_____

_____

_____

_____

_____

_____

_____

_____

_____

_____

Maintaining a Sacred Relationship

walking the path

⟶

It is called a path because you
are meant to walk it.

~NATIVE AMERICAN PROVERB

The work of creating and maintaining the relationship that you desire begins now. This book has supported your learning and practicing thus far, but now is the time for you to put your plan into action and make lasting changes.

The results from our Sacred Relationship retreats are clear—couples who put their plans into practice change their lives and achieve new levels of love, healing, and connection. However, those couples who do not take up the practices fall back into the same patterns and stories as when they began this work, with little or no improvement. The choice is yours.

YOURSELF

The single most important factor in creating a Sacred Relationship with your beloved is to tend to your own personal vibration. If you are living in the vibratory depths of anger, frustration, anxiety, and resentment, there is no possible way for you to feed loving, supportive, and nurturing energy to your beloved.

Use the healing and uplifting work that you have done so far as a foundation for further growth. Take your personal practices seriously, and prioritize your own self-care and development. There will always be a storm of demands on your time and attention from children, partner, job, family, and friends. However, what could be more important than developing your body and mind to be able to hold the love and light that will uplift you?

While it may sound quaint, the path to happiness, inner peace, and a magnificent, loving relationship begins with exercising every day, eating a healthy diet, avoiding toxins of all types, and focusing on raising your personal vibration through continued learning and personal practices.

THE COUPLE

The start of your journey as a couple living your Sacred Relationship is to do your relationship practices everyday. These will be the cornerstone of your work in raising the vibration of your connection. The tests will come swiftly and steadily, so these practices will develop critical skills for weathering the storms with fresh eyes and with the pillars of love, joy, compassion, and empathy guiding your way.

When you and your beloved feel great and are in a space of love, it is easy to give high-vibration energy to each other. The upward-spiraling cycle of high vibration happens naturally when the give-and-take starts and ends with love. However, it is also easy to go the other way.

For example, let's say you come home feeling angry and frustrated from something that happened at work, and then feed that toxic-junk vibration to your beloved. Chances are that they will feel sick and yucky as a result. This catches them off-guard, and if their resolve is not strong or if they drop their conscious awareness, they will react in low vibration. This in turn upsets you even more, creating that downward spiral of interactions that will likely end in a heated argument.

We want to eliminate this, of course, so the key is to break the downward cycle and shift the energy back toward love, joy, compassion, and empathy. This can only happen if you are utilizing daily practices to keep you living in presence and wholeness with love as your foundation for all your interactions in the world.

HEART WORK: *Dedicate Yourself to Love*

In Anni's and my relationship, we have both gone through a great deal of healing and growth to break through these negativity-reinforcing cycles that plagued us. Having done this work, I can say that the most important aspect that needed to shift in me to access higher vibration was letting go of my ego and pride.

A typical interaction would begin with me making some sort of thoughtless joke or statement that would not feel good to Anni. She would respond from hurt, annoyance, or even anger. I would then begin to defend myself, either by telling her, "I didn't say that," or "I didn't mean it that way," or often, "Well, that's not as bad as the time you said —————!" By now we are deep in our habit bodies, judging each other and already deciding who is right and who is wrong without truly listening to each other.

After I made my vow to Anni to love her unconditionally at the highest vibration possible every day for the rest of my life, my usual response was no longer on the table. Real change came as I was able to drop my prideful, defensive responses and admit, "I am wrong," or "I hear that my words hurt you, and I am sorry." As with everything, practice makes perfect. The first time we stepped into this dynamic again, I became conscious of my vows, stopped being defensive, and began to take my higher road.

This lasted for about three seconds, until my ego pulled me right back down again. But the next time, I held it for three minutes, and so on. I am able to now practice this with reverence and a disciplined mind that starts and ends with how much I love her.

Our message is simple: be only love as you approach your beloved in your relationship. Some things that can get in the way of this are 1) bad habits, 2) your own unhealed wounds that cause low-vibration reactions, and 3) ego and pride that prevent you from going first in taking responsibility and showing compassion. Therefore, as you go forward in your lives together, please continue to do your daily practices to create new habits, do the release and healing work for yourself and for your beloved, and let go of pride so that you can apologize and hear, with deep compassion, what your beloved is saying to you.

IDEAS AND PRACTICES

Take a time-out

Make an agreement with your beloved that any time you begin to have an argument or play out old destructive patterns, you will stop and take a break. When you realize that is happening, you can say something like this: "Honey, you are my one true love, and I do not want to fight with you. Let us take a few moments to breathe together so that I can come back to you in love, compassion, and humility."

Then sit together and do deep-breathing together, in through your nose and out through your mouth. As you breathe together, say the following mantras:

Breathing in, I see you before me.

Breathing out, I recognize that you are my love.

Breathing in, I see you before me.

Breathing out, I see that you are in pain.

Breathing in, I see you before me.

Breathing out, I want to understand the cause of your pain.

Breathing in, I see you before me.

Breathing out, I want to ease your pain.

pairings

- Altar centerpiece. We have already written about the importance of creating a Sacred Space in your home, and of creating a Relationship Altar. As you complete the journey of this book and embark upon the next stage of your relationship journey, find a dramatic centerpiece for your Relationship Altar. It could be a statue, a large crystal, or any significant item that you find in nature such as an amazing stick or seashell. Go out together and find something that speaks deeply to both of you. This piece will be a daily reminder to you of the Sacred Relationship that you want, and the commitments that you both have made to manifest your refreshed connection.

Journal on Maintaining A Sacred Relationship

Use this space to reflect on the journey that you have taken together through this book. What have you learned? What do you see differently? How will you be able to go forward to create your own Sacred Relationship?

_____

_____

_____

_____

_____

_____

_____

_____

_____

_____

_____

_____

_____

_____

_____

_____

_____

ABOUT THE AUTHORS

 ANNI DAULTER is the author of *Sacred Pregnancy, Sacred Motherhood,* and *Sacred Medicine Cupboard* and is the founder of the Sacred Living Movement. She travels the world leading retreats that inspire, uplift, and connect women in many areas of their lives. Daulter trains birth workers to lead Sacred Pregnancy classes, helps couples heal at Sacred Relationship retreats, empowers women at I AM Sisterhood retreats, and brings moms and daughters together in celebration at Sacred Sweeties retreats. She lives with her husband and four children in Boulder, Colorado.

 TIM DAULTER, a native of Philadelphia, earned a BS in both Chemical Engineering and Engineering and Public Policy from Carnegie Mellon University and a PhD in Chemical Engineering from the University of Delaware. Six years of working as an engineer for the DuPont Company finally convinced him that he was on the wrong path. As a result of many personal awakenings he ventured to California where he earned an MBA from Pepperdine University.

After meeting his wife Anni and the birth of their first child together, they were inspired to create an organic baby food company. This experience proved both rewarding and challenging, and although he valued the lessons he received, Daulter knew that his calling was for a more spiritual life. He began to discover the spiritual teachings that further deepened his spark of self awareness and led him down a path of self improvement and spiritual growth that has given him the greatest gift of all—the ability to be happy. He wrote a popular self-healing book, *Practicing Happy: A Spiritual Workout for Happiness and Fulfillment in Your Life,* which is a practical guide to help the reader find his/her happiness in life.

Although he has sometimes been a reluctant student in learning and living the principles laid out in this book, the stunning transformation that he experienced over a period of a few years inspired him to share the gifts that were given to him with as many people as possible.

The Daulters are happily married soulmates and adore their four children: Zoë, Lotus Sunshine, Bodhi Ocean, and River Love. They currently lead Sacred Relationship Retreats together all around the world.

PHOTOGRAPHY CREDITS

Thank you to all the photographers who contributed to *Sacred Relationship* and made it the beautiful book that it is! We love every picture and feel very grateful to each and every photographer. Their images bring this book to life for everyone.

COVER:
Trevor and MacK Mars of SoulMakes, on their wedding day.
The photo is by Sarah Loven of Ready Gypset Go.
www.readygypsetgo.com

The wedding couple and photographers realized they had a common thread of living an art-full life and were inspired to create beautiful images for such a special wedding event. The cover photo was taken hours after the wedding, long after everyone else had left, and the four of them wandered and explored the nearby woods and took photos until the sun went down. The cover photo was one of the last taken, during dusk, after a long day of celebration of love, on a mountain in Frederick, Maryland.

SECTION 1: WE REFLECT

Jane Ferrell, Jane in the Woods

www.janeinthewoods.com

WEEK 1: SWOON

The Blissful Maven

Candice Zugich

theblissfulmaven@gmail.com

www.theblissfulmaven.com

WEEK 2: SOUL CONTRACTS

Danica Donnelly Photography

www.danicadonnelly.com

WEEK 3: HEART WORK

Ashley Johnson

WEEK 4: BEGINNER'S MIND

Camilla Albano-Fotografia

www.flickr.com/photos/camilla_albano

WEEK 5: PILLOW TALK

Jane Ferrell

Jane in the Woods

www.janeinthewoods.com

WEEK 6: HEALING WOUNDS

Camilla Albano-Fotografia

www.flickr.com/photos/camilla_albano

WEEK 7: TRUST

Jane Ferrell

Jane in the Woods

www.janeinthewoods.com

WEEK 8: LOVE'S NECTAR

Heidi Marie Wagstaff

www.truefeather.net

Styling: Anni Daulter/Delicious Gratitude

SECTION 2: WE PRACTICE

Jane Ferrell

Jane in the Woods

www.janeinthewoods.com

WEEK 9: LOVE WARRIOR

Christopher Soloma de Cadavid

Squirrel Films

SquirrelFilms.com

WEEK 10: IT'S ALL ABOUT
THE ENERGY
Christopher Soloma de Cadavid
Squirrel Films
SquirrelFilms.com

WEEK 11: DIVINE MIND
Zipporah Lomax
http://zipporahlomax.com

WEEK 12: SPEAK MY
LANGUAGE
Jane Ferrell
Jane in the Woods
www.janeinthewoods.com

WEEK 13: FIVE DAILY
PRACTICES
Heidi Marie Wagstaff
www.truefeather.net

WEEK 14: WORD MEDICINE
Myrriah Jannett
Peaceful Birth Haven
www.peacefulbirthhaven.com

WEEK 15: NAKED TIME
The Blissful Maven
Candice Zugich
theblissfulmaven@gmail.com
www.theblissfulmaven.com

WEEK 16: SEX
Ingrid Pullen
http://ingridpullenphotography.com.au
/coming-soon
www.facebook.com/ingridpullen
photography

SECTION 3: WE ENVISION
Jane Ferrell
Jane in the Woods
www.janeinthewoods.com

WEEK 17: TAKING STOCK
Zipporah Lomax
http://zipporahlomax.com

WEEK 18: SPIRITUAL
DIVORCE
Jane Ferrell
Jane in the Woods
www.janeinthewoods.com

WEEK 19: BROTHERHOOD
Christopher Soloma de Cadavid
Squirrel Films
SquirrelFilms.com

WEEK 20: SISTERHOOD
Camilla Albano-Fotografia
www.flickr.com/photos/camilla_albano

WEEK 21: CEREMONIAL
MIND
The Visionary Photographic Art
of Chanel Baran
www.ChanelBaran.com
Facilitator—Fire Mane
www.pachartakiyperutours.com

WEEK 22: RELEASE IT
The Visionary Photographic Art
of Chanel Baran
www.ChanelBaran.com

WEEK 23: ROMANCE ME
Jane Ferrell
Jane in the Woods
www.janeinthewoods.com

WEEK 24: FAMILY FOLD
Bobbi-lee Hille of Blee
Photography
Milyali Art project
www.perthbaby.com.au

SECTION 4: WE VOW
Jane Ferrell
Jane in the Woods
www.janeinthewoods.com

WEEK 25: SPIRIT GUIDES
Myrriah Jannett
Peaceful Birth Haven
www.peacefulbirthhaven.com

WEEK 26: SPIRITUAL MIND
Camilla Albano-Fotografia
www.flickr.com/photos/camilla_albano

WEEK 27: REMOVING FAIR
Ingrid Pullen
*http://ingridpullenphotography.com.au
/coming-soon*
*www.facebook.com/ingridpullen
photography*

WEEK 28: LOVE MANDALA
Anni Daulter
www.sacredlivingmovement.com
Shot taken at a Sacred
Relationship Retreat

WEEK 29: SACRED
AGREEMENTS
Jane Ferrell
Jane in the Woods
www.janeinthewoods.com

WEEK 30: SALT BOWL
INTENTIONS
Heidi Marie Wagstaff
www.truefeather.net
Styling: Anni Daulter/Delicious
Gratitude

WEEK 31: BEAUTY WAY
CEREMONY
Jane Ferrell
Jane in the Woods
www.janeinthewoods.com

WEEK 32: MAINTAINING A
SACRED RELATIONSHIP
The Blissful Maven
Candice Zugich
theblissfulmaven@gmail.com
www.theblissfulmaven.com

TITLES BY ANNI DAULTER

available from North Atlantic Books

Sacred Pregnancy

978-1-58394-462-2

Sacred Motherhood

978-1-62317-004-2

Sacred Medicine Cupboard

978-1-62317-068-4

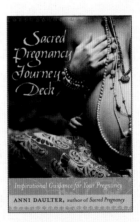

Sacred Pregnancy
Journey Deck

978-1-62317-134-6

North Atlantic Books
www.northatlanticbooks.com

North Atlantic Books is an independent, nonprofit publisher committed to a bold exploration of the relationships between mind, body, spirit, and nature.

About North Atlantic Books

North Atlantic Books (NAB) is an independent, nonprofit publisher committed to a bold exploration of the relationships between mind, body, spirit, and nature. Founded in 1974, NAB aims to nurture a holistic view of the arts, sciences, humanities, and healing. To make a donation or to learn more about our books, authors, events, and newsletter, please visit www.northatlanticbooks.com.

For more information on books, authors, events, and to sign up for our newsletter, please visit www.northatlanticbooks.com.

North Atlantic Books is the publishing arm of the Society for the Study of Native Arts and Sciences, a 501(c)(3) nonprofit educational organization that promotes cross-cultural perspectives linking scientific, social, and artistic fields. To learn how you can support us, please visit our website.